WEAVING CONTEMPORARY RAG RUGS

WEAVING CONTEMPORARY RAG RUGS

NEW DESIGNS ■ TRADITIONAL TECHNIQUES

Heather L. Allen

Lark Books

50 College Street, Asheville, NC 28801

Dedication

Dedicated to the memory of my Finnish grandmother, Alma Hietala Allen,
and to my friend and mentor Barbara Ekchardt

Editor: Leslie Dierks
Art Director: Dana Irwin
Photography: As noted; all photos not credited are by Evan Bracken
Illustrations: Kay Holmes Stafford
Computer-Generated Artwork: Bobby Gold
Production: Dana Irwin

Allen, Heather, 1963-
     Weaving contemporary rag rugs : new designs, traditional techniques / Heather L. Allen. -- 1st ed.
          p. cm.
     Includes bibliographic references and index.
     ISBN 1-887374-39-6
     1. Rag rugs. 2. Hand weaving.   I. Title.
TT850.A415   1998
  746.7'2--dc21   97-19740
                                                            CIP

10 9 8 7 6 5 4 3 2 1

First Edition

Published by Lark Books
50 College Street
Asheville, North Carolina 28801, USA

Distributed by Random House, Inc., in the United States, Canada,
   the United Kingdom, Europe, and Asia

Distributed in Australia by Capricorn Link (Australia) Pty Ltd.,
   P.O. Box 6651, Baulkham Hills Business Centre, NSW 2153, Australia

Distributed in New Zealand by Tandem Press Ltd., 2 Rugby Rd.,
   Birkenhead, Auckland, New Zealand

Printed in Hong Kong

1-887374-39-6

CONTENTS

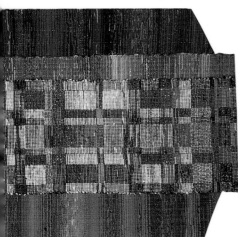

INTRODUCTION

Fabric and color have always had a special place in my life. Near my home in Asheville, North Carolina, there is a Goodwill store that I love to visit. In the front of the store, clothing is displayed on circular racks by color—a circle of red, orange, and magenta shirts next to a circle of blue and green ones. I love to see these colored fabrics next to each other! Whenever I'm in an environment that is filled with glorious colors, my energy level soars.

Long before I became a textile artist, I was a fabric collector. Perhaps a more appropriate term would be a fabric hoarder, since I rarely discard a piece of cloth, no matter how small. As a child I had a box of prized fabric scraps that I would pore over, sorting and touching, examining and rearranging. To me scraps of cloth are not generic; they contain personal histories that reflect specific people and their lives. Laden with memories of people, places, and

events, fabrics can be as evocative as photographs, conjuring up stories and images from the past.

In my home I have rag rugs that incorporate worn-out clothing from myself, my family, and my friends. I recently wove a rug that contains a favorite plaid flannel shirt from my adolescence. An unusual combination of bright reds and teals, that shirt was worn until no more mending could sustain it. Recently I had need for those colors, and now my precious shirt lives on as a familiar stripe in a rag rug on my floor. This rug and others speak volumes about the intimacy associated with cloth as a part of daily life. They speak also of the process of collecting and saving, of the stories, associations, and memories contained in the reused cloth.

Like quilts, rag rugs serve as a form of social commentary, reflecting the materials of the culture from which they come. In decades past, the limited palette found in rag rugs mirrored the clothing worn at the time; today there are very few limitations on the palette or the available materials.

In our modern, high-tech world of metal, plastics, and videos, the act of weaving a rug provides a connection to a simpler lifestyle. Virtually unchanged over the centuries, rag weaving is a manual process that is demanding both physically and mentally. At the same time, it is spiritually rejuvenating. Recycling society's remnants and castoffs into rugs

Weaving a rag rug is an auditory as well as a tactile experience. The soft music of the loom creates a wonderful atmosphere, and the process of weaving rag rugs is similar to having a conversation—a rapport develops between the weaver, the fabrics, and the design. The conversation evolves and unfolds as the rug is woven on the loom; the rhythm of the loom audibly echoes the progress as the shuttles fly like thoughts and the beater responds.

The idea for this book began while I was in graduate school and was just beginning to explore the

that are beautiful and functional yields a wonderful feeling of accomplishment. Rag weaving also instills a sense of connection, of being interwoven with history and tradition.

ABOVE:
Adagio,
Raili Ruppa
(Finnish), 67" x
94½" (170 x 240
cm), cotton
warp and weft
PHOTO: KARL LAHTI

ABOVE RIGHT:
Saki-ori obis
("torn-woven
sashes") from
Japan, artists
unknown,
9¼" x 140"
(23.5 x 356
cm), cotton
warp and weft,
from the collec-
tion of Jorie
Johnson
PHOTO: KOICHI
NISHIMURA

creative potential of the woven rag rug. I had found several books that contained wonderful technical information but none that dealt with the creative aspects of rag rug weaving. During that time, I attended the session of Convergence—the bienni-al conference of the Handweaver's Guild of America—that focused on rag rugs. At the rag rug "show and tell," Paula Pfaff, a noted weaver and coauthor of the *Rag Rug Handbook*, showed a very unusual rug from Finland that employed surface design techniques. At the same conference I learned of an exhibition at the San Francisco Craft and Folk Art Museum of *saki-ori,* a traditional form of rag weaving from Japan. The beautiful catalog that accompanied the *saki-ori* exhibit and my sub-sequent contacts with Raili Ruppa, the Finnish weaver whose striking rug had captured my imagi-nation, inspired me to learn more about the rag rug traditions in various parts of the world.

Rag rugs have been integral to the evolution of weaving and floor coverings in many countries, yet they are neglected in most history books. If addressed at all, rag rugs are given only scanty attention. This treatment implies that rag rugs aren't worthy of a more complete documentation. Does the term *rag* carry a stigma? In our affluent Western society, the word has negative connotations (Webster's defines it as a *waste* piece of cloth), but in Buddhist philosophy, old materials that have been patched and repaired are signs of humility and are valued far more highly than something that is new.

For centuries people have woven rag rugs to fulfill their needs and desires, and these same needs and desires inspire today's weavers. It is my hope that when the history books of today are written, rag rugs will have their rightful place in them.

Historically rag rugs have been practical and func-tional, adhering to the classic phrase "form follows function," but the natural evolution of the craft has led to greater experimentation in designs, weave patterns, and color schemes. Although traditional rag rugs continue to fulfill a need for beautiful and functional floor coverings, contemporary weavers are also exploring the unknown, using symbolic content and less conventional materials and tech-niques.

Some contemporary rag rugs address environmen-tal and political concerns. Weavers of these rugs look at their collection of rags and societal rem-nants from a different perspective—they see the symbolic content and the social commentary of the rags themselves. These rugs do not conform to the typical image of a rag rug, but they are won-derful and exciting developments.

Canadian weaver Wendy Bateman is an avid envi-ronmentalist, and she feels a strong commitment to the recycling aspect of rag rugs. In 1991 she and Sid Brinkman created *Recycled Sweat Lodge,* a wil-low frame that is covered with seven 14-foot (4.3-meter) rag blankets woven from 4,000 plastic gro-cery bags. Sitting inside the sweat lodge with the

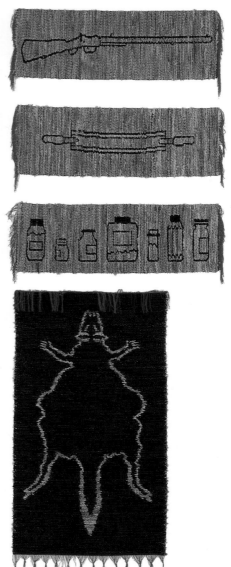

entrance flap closed, a person experiences a feeling of suffocation. *Recycled Sweat Lodge* conveys Wendy's impression of what the Earth is experiencing from our excessive waste. The lodge has been used educationally as a means of enlightening school children about the ill effects of our current disposable society.

Beth Hatton, who lives in Annandale, Australia, is a long time weaver of recycled materials. In addition to her more traditional rag rugs (see her project in chapter 6), she has done a series of rugs incorporating discarded bits of kangaroo skin. These remnants are a result of culling the native kangaroo population to preserve land for imported domestic animals. Like *Recycled Sweat Lodge*, these rag rugs raise questions concerning the impact of society on the natural world. Through their use of consumer waste, Wendy Bateman and Beth Hatton create rag rugs that are powerful social statements.

There are as many types of rag rugs as there are weavers. This book includes both the traditional and the contemporary. Some weavers warp their looms, then design their rugs. Others, sitting amidst an array of warp and rags, design spontaneously from their materials. Another group starts with an idea, concept, or message and then determines the materials and techniques. There is neither a stereotypical nor an ultimate rag rug; instead, there are endless possibilities. With this book, I hope to inspire your creativity and to encourage you to look to the past for guidance while exploring the limitless potential of the future.

For me the path and the process are more important than the outcome.....Change, moment to moment....Breathing in breathing out. Warp up weft down. Their intersection is the present.

BHAKTI ZIEK

1

HISTORICAL PERSPECTIVE

The tradition of weaving with fragmented strips of cloth began among the poorer classes at a time in history when cloth was treasured, and mending and patching were meticulously done to extend the life of every textile. It is difficult to imagine now, but cloth was once so scarce and highly valued that it was often unwoven for the thread itself. Thus, weaving with rags as a weft did not evolve out of technological advance or discovery; instead it developed out of frugality, ingenuity, and genuine necessity.

Rag blanket of the Merina people of Madagascar, 33"x87½" (84 x 222 cm) woven of colorless plastic fibers (warp) and scraps and off-cuts of waste cotton (weft)

known rag weaving traditions, documentation began in the 1700s. In general, this documentation occurred only after rag weaving traditions had made their way from the peasant to the wealthier classes. Estate listings, old portraits by itinerant painters, letters, and diaries document the early history of rag weaving.

Rag-Woven Bedding & Coverlets

By necessity, weaving rags into sturdy, warm cloth to be used for bedding or clothing predates the weaving of rags into rugs. In the 1700s, the Swedish peasant class wove all of their everyday textiles. Generally made of linen or wool, these textiles were highly valued because they represented a considerable investment of time and energy. Clothing was painstakingly patched and mended to extend its life, then used as raw materials for rag weaving.

A typical Swedish peasant home had one open, multipurpose room with simple straw or hay mattress beds. Early rag weavings—*underbreda*—served as

Due to their utilitarian nature, early examples of rag weaving no longer exist, and the date of the earliest rag weaving is not known. The oldest remnant in North America is a small rag-woven blanket fragment from the prehistoric Salado culture that lived in the Tonto Basin, Roosevelt, Arizona, during 1100 to 1400 A.D. In countries with better-

sturdy, impenetrable bottom sheets that covered the straw mattresses. Also common were rag-woven bedspreads, referred to as tatter coverlets or *slarvklade*. These early rag blankets were made of two narrow widths of plain weave or twill that were sewn together. The palette for these rag weavings was limited to natural shades of white, brown, grey, and black, which reflected the everyday linen and wool clothes worn in Sweden at the time.

Although there doesn't seem to have been a rag-woven bedding tradition in the American colonies, there was a coverlet tradition in neighboring Canada. Similar in climate to Scandinavia, the long, harsh winters of Canada encouraged the early settlers of the eastern provinces to develop a tradition of rag coverlets that remained popular into the 20th century. These coverlets were referred to as *catalogne* in areas of Quebec and *cloutie* in Scottish settlements.

Woven rag coverlets held a very special place of honor among the French Acadians of the Maritime provinces and Quebec. Acadian mothers wove a trousseau for every daughter, and among the many textiles of the trousseau were the *couvertures de marriage* or bridal coverlets. Some were woven of white rags that had been saved for years, until a suf-

ficient amount had been accumulated to weave into a coverlet.

During the 1760–70s, the British took possession of Canada and expelled anyone who would not raise arms against France. Many Acadians took refuge in French-speaking Louisiana, where they maintained their cultural identity well into the 20th century. Among the traditions they brought with them was the rag-woven coverlet.

In northern Japan, weaving with narrow strips of cloth began in the 1750s. Until this time, peasants from many rural northern areas depended on the fiber from the bast plant for their clothing. The coarse cloth made from bast fibers was extremely durable but did not afford much warmth in the harsh winters. In order to obtain a warmer fiber at an affordable cost, peasants began to buy cotton

rags in bundles from merchants from southern port towns.

The cotton rags were woven on a backstrap loom, using a heavy beater, to make narrow strips of a tightly woven cloth called *saki-ori.* The strips of saki-ori were sewn into *yogi*—long, heavy, kimono-like housecoats that were worn as garments during the day, then used as bedding at night.

Another important rag weaving tradition in Japan is the *kotatsugake,* a heavy coverlet that is placed over a *kotatsu,* the traditional device used for heating a Japanese home. Members of the family sit around the kotatsu with their hands and feet placed under the kotatsugake for warmth. Long strips of saki-ori were sewn together to make the kotatsugake. Though smaller in scale, kotatsugakes strongly resemble the rag carpets of North America and

Sweden that were made from long strips of rag weaving sewn together, and in rural areas kotatsugakes were sometimes used on the floor as rugs. To a westerner they would seem too delicate to be a floor covering, but in an environment where shoes are removed upon entering a home, a lighter weight weaving is adequate.

Rag Weavings for the Floor

The evolution of rag weaving is linked to that of the house. As the standard of living increased and houses grew larger, rag rugs moved from the bed to the table to the floor.

Long traditions of temporary or seasonal floor decoration created an environment receptive to floor coverings and rugs. In Sweden, floors were strewn with such things as straw, spruce needles, aspen

FAR LEFT:
Ticking,
Ingela Norén
(Swedish), 30" x
60" (76 x 152.5
cm), 12/6 cotton
warp and cotton
weft
PHOTO: INGELA NORÉN

LEFT:
Autumn Fields,
Gulvi Heed
(Swedish), 24¾"
x 94½" (63 x 240
cm), cotton yarn
warp, cotton yarn
and rye straw
weft, ribbed with
cotton ribbon
PHOTO: HANS
KONGBÄCK

BELOW:
Selection of rag
rugs woven based
on the collection
at the Nordiska
Museum in
Stolkholm,
Sweden, Gullvi
Heed (Swedish),
various sizes and
materials
PHOTO: HANS
KONGBÄCK

leaves, and flowers on religious occasions and other times of ritual. This tradition moved to the U.S., and on special occasions in colonial New England, wooden floors were well scoured and strewn with clean white sand. When guests were expected, the sand was swept into decorative patterns.

The earliest woven floor coverings in both Sweden and New England were made with straw wefts, which were later combined with rag strips. In the beginning, the weft included any bits of available material—rags, fabric scraps, emptied flour sacks, fishing nets, and bits of string.

The first rag rugs were highly prized and reserved for use on holidays or for other special events. In his article, "The American Rag Carpet: A Rags-to-Riches Story" (*Country Living*, November 1985), Victor Weinblatt states that "...a rag carpet would

be used to line the path of the spring procession of the blessing of the crops. Sometimes over a hundred feet long, the carpet would be unrolled from the front steps of the church out into the fields. The priest would then lead the congregation out from the church over the carpet...." Such carpets

were as highly prized as heirloom china, and because they were often used only once a year, they remained in excellent condition.

As the standard of living improved in the first half of the 19th century, houses gained more rooms, such as parlors and drawing rooms, where prized rag rugs could be kept out of the way of everyday traffic. By the mid–19th century, rag rugs became commonplace on many floors in the house.

The discovery of aniline dyes in 1856 caused the physical appearance of rag rugs to change dramatically all over the world. The earlier palette, consisting of subtle shades of white, black, indigo, and other natural colors, was replaced with a full spectrum of vivid commercial hues. As industrialization took hold, rag weaving continued to increase in popularity and expand in scope and color.

Rag rugs have historically been woven on beautiful, heavy, two- or four-shaft looms that were built by hand. In the U.S. and in Scandinavian countries, these looms were often collectively owned and shared. Many of the looms in colonial America were constructed based on memories of those used in Europe.

During the latter part of the 19th century, a number of commercial loom manufacturers were established in America in response to the demands of a growing home textile industry. Weaving rag rugs had become a profitable cottage industry for men and women across the country, and many looms were engineered specifically for producing rag rugs in the home. While remaining sturdy in construction, these looms were made more compact and collapsible to suit smaller domestic spaces.

The terms *rag rug* and *rag carpeting* are often used interchangeably, but rug generally refers to a smaller floor covering, and carpet refers to a large floor covering. Although some looms could weave extremely wide, seamless rugs, rag carpeting was

generally woven in long strips between 26 and 36 inches (66 and 91.5 cm) wide—similar to yard goods—then cut and used individually or sewn together to fit the intended location.

This cutting and arranging is a wonderful aspect of rag rugs. In addition to their use as area rugs, they could be laid in strips next to each other to cover an entire floor, sometimes overlapping a little to make sweeping easier. In Sweden long strips were often used in hallways and arranged in patterns around tables. They could be picked up and moved around, so they were easy to clean and tended to wear evenly. In some instances, to make a more permanent floor covering, rag rugs were tacked or nailed in place.

Rag rugs remained popular in America until the turn of the century, when linoleum was introduced. At first linoleum was expensive, and a small piece was treated like a prized area rug. It was often placed under a table and surrounded by rag rugs. In

high-traffic areas, rag rugs were often laid on top of the linoleum to protect the more valuable surface. As the cost of linoleum decreased, its popularity and usage increased. In the 1960s came the onslaught of wall-to-wall carpeting, and the rag rug was relegated to the back hall or kitchen. Not surprisingly, during these years many loom manufacturers liquidated, and looms across the country were dismantled and put away in barns or basements and forgotten.

More recently, the infatuation with linoleum and wall-to-wall carpeting has worn off. Many people are removing these now dated floor coverings and rediscovering the beauty and charm of hardwood

floors. With the reemergence of the wooden floor has come an increased interest in smaller floor coverings, including rag rugs. Interest and demand are also promoted by the numerous examples of ongoing historical renovation. Once again rag rugs are valued and enjoyed as beautiful floor coverings fit for any room of the house.

Rag Rugs Today

Although the basics of rag rug weaving have remained the same over the years, the materials have changed significantly. The first rag rug weavers had a very limited palette and selection of fabrics. Nowadays there is an abundant array of warps and fabrics, with a diversity of fiber content, color, and pattern. In addition, through fabric dyeing and other manipulation, contemporary weavers can transform fabrics however they please. Recycled woven and knit fabrics, industrial cast-offs, plastic bread wrappers, shopping bags, and nylon stockings have all found their way into rugs.

There are many variations in fabrics, designs, palettes, and uses for rag rugs around the world. Throughout Africa, men traditionally do the weaving on treadle looms, and in Egypt, rag rugs are woven by men in small one- or two-person shops. The looms and the weaving knowledge are passed down from father to son, and in Egyptian homes, mothers and daughters prepare the rags for weaving. Generally striped and colorful, their palettes are dictated by the surplus that is available for purchase from mechanized weaving or clothing industries. Indicative of the value of rag rugs in contemporary life is the fact that rag-woven fabric is currently very popular in Egypt for covering car seats.

Employment and empowerment coalesce in rag rugs. The raw materials necessary for making them are comparatively cheap, and weaving them is not hard to learn—all you need are looms, a teacher, and some willing individuals. A wonderful example is Stefan Bengtsson, who was born in Sweden and grew up on a mission station in South Africa. Inspired by memories of the Swedish rag rugs he had grown up with as a child, he and his wife began a rag rug cottage industry in South Africa. He located two dismantled Swedish floor looms and established Kingdom Weavers to provide much-needed employment and income to Zulu mothers. They weave Swedish-style striped rag rugs, using waste fabric from the local T-shirt industry.

In southern Norway a similar cooperative was formed to provide work for a group of unemployed women. In 1991, under the direction of Eva Nyhus, RuterDame was formed by nine women in Risor, Norway. The women were trained in production weaving and hoped to fulfill a need in Norway for handwoven rugs. Their cotton rags are knitted or woven and are industrially dyed and stripped for them. Inspired by traditional Norwegian weave patterns such as Rosepath and various twills, their rugs are woven using a modern palette and perspective.

Today in Finland there are nearly 200 centers sponsored by the Finnish Crafts and Arts Organizations where people can weave. Rag rugs have a long history in Finland, and the organization helps to keep this tradition alive.

In addition to the traditional linen or seine twine warp, Finland has a history of using a very strong paper yarn to weave upholstery fabric. This paper yarn is being used in rag rugs by a young Finnish designer, Hanna Korvela. There is an old Finnish saying that a well-woven rug should be able to stand on end. With her rag rugs, Hanna is maintaining that age-old tradition. She, like RuterDame and many others, illustrates a new breed of rag rug weaver who works with interior designers and corporate spaces.

In the past, scarcity, frugality, and necessity were the driving forces behind rag rug weaving. These remain strong motivating factors today, but there is also a growing appreciation of the artistic value of rag rugs by contemporary artists from all over the world. As the role of the rag rug evolves, so does its appearance. Rag rugs are now part of the interior design repertoire, appearing in posh commercial interiors as well as in the common homes where they have always been loved and appreciated. And while there is still plenty of charm in the traditional striped and Hit-and-Miss rag rugs, there are also infinite possibilities waiting to be discovered.

LEFT:
Panama Med Prikk Og Kjerringtenner, woven at Veveriet RuterDame by Eva Nyhus, large rug is 67" x 95½" (170 x 240 cm), smaller rugs are 31½" x 98½" (80 x 250 cm), basket weave or twill with inlay, 12/6 cotton warp and cotton weft
PHOTO: DANNEVIG FOTO

BELOW:
Duetto carpet selection, Hannah Korvela (Finnish), plain weave, paper string warp and cotton weft
PHOTO: PEKKA MÄKINEN

II

TOOLS & MATERIALS

Not only are rag rugs beautiful to have in your home, but they are also exciting to weave. The basics are easy to learn and the creative potential endless. The materials consist of warp and fabric, and with the exception of the loom, rag rug weaving requires only very basic tools. This chapter describes these tools and their purpose. If you're unfamiliar with any of the terms as they are used here, refer to the glossary on page 122.

RIGHT:
Trio of warp windings and assortment of warp thread

Warp Thread

Warp thread is available in many fibers, colors, and strengths. Colored warp can add a wonderful design element if your sett is 10 or 12 epi. Using a sett of 5 or 6 results in a rug that is weft faced, and the warp is essentially hidden, making the choice of color less significant. Rugs woven at low epi's should be double sleyed or woven with a good, strong warp such as seine twine or a double-twisted warp for added strength.

Warp thread is classified by a numbered fraction that signifies size and ply. The numerator indicates the fineness of the individual strand, and the denominator represents the number of strands that are twisted together (ply) to make the thread. A higher figure in the numerator indicates a finer strand. The weight and strength of a particular warp thread depends upon the size of the strand, the number of plies, and its fiber content. Some of the most commonly available warp threads are:

■ 5/2 mercerized cotton: luxurious but not as sturdy as heavier warps

■ 8/4 cotton carpet warp: very sturdy; available in a wide variety of colors; good for 10 or 12 epi; inexpensive and the most commonly used

■ 8/4 50/50 polyester-cotton warp: strong and slightly heavier than 8/4 cotton carpet warp

■ Polyester and frayless warp: very strong but limited in color selection

- Seine twine: very durable; natural colored; often used with a sett of 5 or 6 epi

- 8/4 or 8/5 linen: very strong; often used with a sett of 5 or 6 epi

Weft

Fabric! Fabric storage can ultimately take up as much space as a loom. I have had many letters from textile artists and other fabric hounds who turned to weaving rag rugs in order to decrease their piles of fabric! You may already have sufficient material for a couple of rugs in the old clothing and fabrics stored away in a back room or closet. For fabric collectors, weaving rag rugs is a pleasurable way to keep fabric under control.

Every fabric is a potential weft, so don't discard any; instead, learn to use each material for its unique properties. Although some fabrics, such as knits, should be woven separately, there is no limit to what you can use. Remember that rag rugs originated out of necessity and frugality; people have been very ingenious at collecting and using a wide variety of weft material over the years. At different points in history, rag rugs have contained wefts of straw, fishing nets, flour sacks, bread wrappers, and nylon stockings to supplement the meager supply of cloth rags.

Your fabric collection will probably maintain itself once family and friends learn of your need. Fabric may even appear unexpectedly on your doorstep. Can rags be considered a gift? Absolutely! When Sidney Brinkman was courting Canadian weaver Wendy Bateman, instead of flowers he presented her with 100-pound bags of Harris Tweed fabric salvaged from his job as a cutter in Toronto. During their first year of courtship, Wendy received about 3,000 pounds of material. Needless to say, the two are now married.

Hunting for bargains and finding the perfect colors can be oodles of fun. Low-cost fabrics can be found at yard sales, flea markets, thrift stores, and in the closets of friends. Become a member of a weaving guild or form a rag rug group. Swap and trade colors; every person has a different color palette, and a color you dislike may be someone else's favorite.

For many rag rug weavers, the recycling of materials is a very important part of the process. Unlike societies in the past where recycling was done because goods were scarce, modern consumer societies encourage recycling to deal with an overabundance of waste. Thus the textile industry itself is a good resource for discarded cloth. Mill ends, which consist of selvages and cuttings from fabric woven in textile mills, are often available for sale. Fabric bolts can be bought and cut with bandsaws

LEFT:
Potential weft fabrics

ABOVE:
Untitled, Susan Johnson (American), 22" x 40" (56 x 101.5 cm), Swedish double-binding weave, velveteen and plastic weft
PHOTO: EVAN BRACKEN

into appropriate widths. If you're looking for large quantities of fabric, check your phone book or the library for local textile manufacturers. Davison's Textile Blue Book and the Thomas Register provide listings of mill remnant and rag dealers. The American Business Disk, a directory available at libraries on CD-rom, also has listings under "textiles." Keep in mind that fabric can be heavy—dealing on a local level is advantageous.

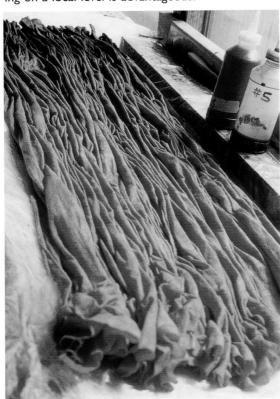

RIGHT:
Gradation-dying of muslin yardage by Wendy Regier (American)
PHOTO: HANNAH REGIER

BELOW:
Dyed sheets and old chenille bedspreads in the studio of Mary Anne Wise (American)
PHOTO: MARY ANNE WISE

Many contemporary rag rug weavers supplement their rags with hand-dyed fabrics and with fabrics purchased specifically for color, pattern, or texture.

It is essential to make sure all your fabric is clean and as free from dirt and excess dye as possible. This is important to rid old fabric or articles of clothing of mildew and other pests that might be present. You also don't want it to shrink after it has been woven. Get in the habit of washing all your fabric in hot water and drying it in the dryer as soon as it comes into your home or studio; then it will all be ready to use.

The Loom

Looms designed specifically for rag rug weaving are very heavy and substantial to facilitate tight packing of the weft. Although it's not necessary to have a specialized loom, weaving rag rugs is energetic work, and you'll need a loom that is well built and sturdy. Make sure that the cloth beam of the loom has ample room between itself and the breast beam so that there is sufficient room to accommodate the bulk of multiple woven rugs. The loom should also create a shed wide enough to allow the large, bulky rag shuttle to pass through. A strong and heavy beater is needed to pack the rag wefts tightly. A metal bar can be attached to add weight and facilitate a good, heavy beat. The wider the warp, the heavier the beater should be.

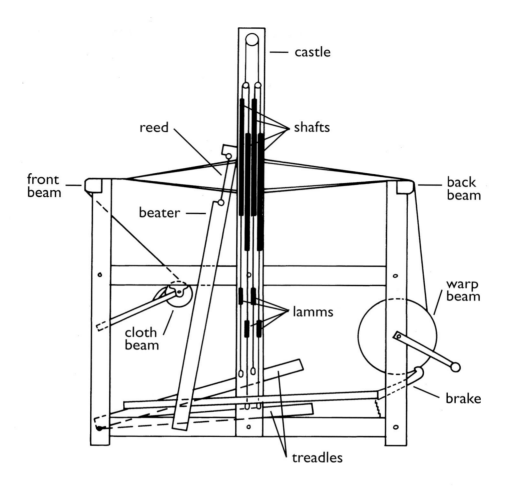

front
beam

reed

castle

shafts

back
beam

beater

cloth
beam

lamms

warp
beam

brake

treadles

Figure 1

A typical loom

Traditional rag rugs were woven on two-shaft looms, but contemporary rag rugs are often woven on looms with four or more, depending on the complexity of the weave.

A loom is a major investment, but bargains can also be found. In addition to the beautiful new looms now available, there are many perfectly wonderful old looms on the market. Rag rug weaving is having a resurgence, yet it has nowhere near the prevalence and popularity it experienced in the late 1800s and early 1900s. There are still many looms remaining from this rag rug heyday. Check newspapers and auction listings or run an advertisement in the weaving periodicals. Let people know you are looking for a loom, and you'll be amazed at what you find. Looms can often be rented through weaving schools and guilds.

Draft

Schematic diagram that provides the necessary information for threading, tie-up, and treadling. They are simple and straightforward, once you understand the basics. It is an international language with slight variations among weavers.

Ends per inch (epi) or sett

An individual warp thread is referred to as an end. The density of a woven cloth or rug is measured by the ends per inch or sett, which is stated as a number. Commonly referred to as the epi, this number indicates how many warp threads there are across one inch of the warp. The sett is the number of threads per inch in the warp and is often used interchangeably with epi. In the United States, 10 or 12 epi is commonly used, which results in rugs that combine warp- and weft-faced elements. When a weft-faced weave is desired, as in many Scandinavian patterns, 5 or 6 epi is used.

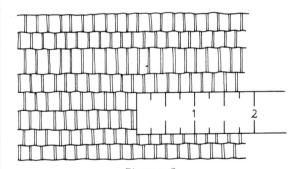

Figure 2

Determining epi (an example of 10 epi)

Filler

The initial material woven into the warp after dressing the loom. This evenly spreads out the warp threads and eliminates the clustering that results from the tie-on process. Heavy rags or rovings of any sort can be used for filler; bulky filler will speed up the process of spreading the warp threads. Double strands of filler are often used for easy removal. Long 1-inch-wide (2.5 cm) strips of cardboard also work very well. They are easy to insert and remove, they're reusable, and they

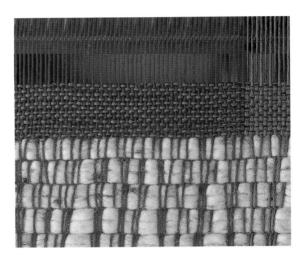

spread out the warp quickly. Filler is also used between two rugs woven on the same warp and to take up the warp that will become fringe or edging after the rug has been cut off the loom.

Header

The area of weaving that comes directly after the filler and thus becomes the beginning of the rug. A header is also woven at the end of the rug. Depending on the finishing treatment, the header can range from ½ to 2 inches (1.5 to 5 cm). The header can be woven with warp threads or thin rags.

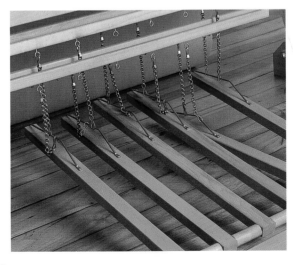

22

Lamms

Narrow wooden beams attached to the shafts. Each lamm can be connected to one or more treadles with rope or chain, allowing the weaver to raise or lower the shafts in various combinations to create weaving patterns. The *tie-up* describes how the lamms are to be attached to the treadles.

Shaft

Shaft refers to the rigid frame that contains the heddles. Looms are often described by the number of shafts they contain. Earlier rag rug looms had two shafts, but now many looms can be purchased as four-shaft looms with room for additional shafts to be installed later. In the U.S., handweavers have used the term *harness* in place of shaft. Technically a harness is a set or group of shafts that work together. The term *shaft* is used in this book.

Shed

The opening created when a certain portion of the warp is lifted or lowered to allow a shuttle to pass through. In the case of rag rugs, an ample shed is necessary for the bulky width of the rag-wrapped shuttle.

23

The force exerted when tightly packing a rag weft often causes the loom to "walk" or to move toward the weaver. Unless your loom is situated on a carpeted surface or a rubber traction pad, it may be necessary to brace it against a wall. This can be done quite simply with two sturdy boards, each wide enough to allow a notch to be cut in one end to fit snugly against the leg of the loom (fig. 3). The other end of each board butts against the wall. A thick rug or pad placed under the loom will help reduce the noise produced during vigorous rug weaving.

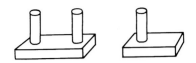

Warping pegs

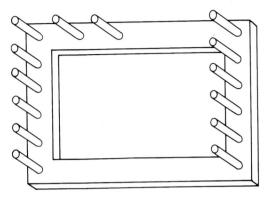

Warping board

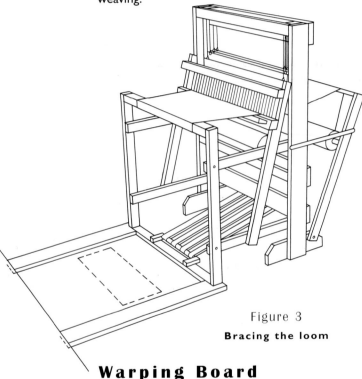

Figure 3

Bracing the loom

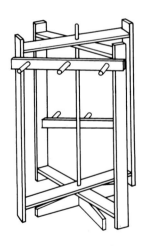

Warping reel

Figure 4

Warping tools

Warping Board

A warping board is a simple frame with pegs attached at convenient locations for measuring out the required length of the warp—*winding* the warp. The warping board allows you to measure long lengths of warp in a very compact way. A warping reel or mill serves the same function, but it allows you to wind longer warps. It also takes up more space. There are stories of weavers winding the warp by running around a barn or tree. The warping board doesn't provide the same aerobic activity, but it does allow you to work year-round regardless of the weather!

Raddle

A raddle is used to space the individual warp threads while winding them onto the loom from back to front. You can easily make a raddle from a narrow wooden board. Cut a piece equal in length to the width of your loom and nail sturdy 2-inch (5-cm) nails along its length at 1- or 2-inch (2.5 or 5-cm) increments.

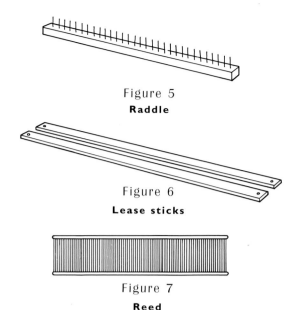

Figure 5
Raddle

Figure 6
Lease sticks

Figure 7
Reed

Lease Sticks

These are two flat wooden slats that generally come with a loom and are usually as long as the loom is wide. They are tied together at each end and used to maintain the warp cross when warping on from back to front.

Reed

The reed spaces the warp threads and packs in the weft. Reeds come in a wide variety of sizes and lengths. They are sized or numbered by how many spaces (called dents) they have per inch. Thus a #12 reed has 12 spaces or dents per inch. In addition to being used as a #12 reed, it can also serve as a #6 by skipping every other dent when sleying.

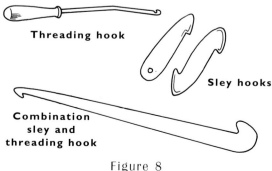

Threading hook

Sley hooks

Combination sley and threading hook

Figure 8
Threading tools

Threading Tools

A threading hook is used to thread the heddles, and the sley or reed hook is used to sley the reed when dressing the loom. Harrisville Designs has a combination sley hook and threading hook all in one tool. You may also prefer to use your fingers for both or either of these tasks.

Shuttles

Weaving rag rugs requires at least two types of shuttles—a rag shuttle and a boat shuttle. Rag shuttles come in three basic styles: ski, rag, and stick, and each comes in assorted sizes. Each style has its advantages, not the least of which is personal preference. A boat shuttle is used for the plain-weave headers, some variations of log cabin, and for creating a ribbed weave effect. Boat shut-

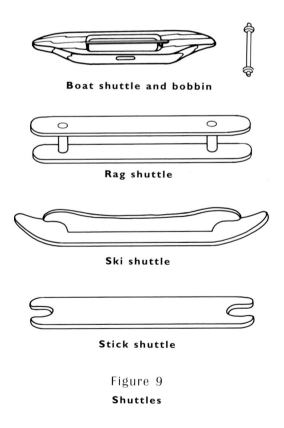

Boat shuttle and bobbin

Rag shuttle

Ski shuttle

Stick shuttle

Figure 9
Shuttles

tles are fitted with individual bobbins or quills that have been loaded with thread using a bobbin winder. Although one or two boat shuttles are sufficient, it's good to have a number of bobbins on hand.

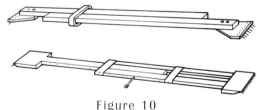

Figure 10

Two types of temples

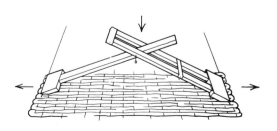

Figure 11

Setting the temple

Temple

A temple is an adjustable stretcher that is used to keep the width of the rug constant and prevent excessive draw-in from occurring. Made of either wood or metal, it has prongs on each end to grip the selvages of the rug. As pressure is applied to the center of the temple, the prongs become embedded in the selvages and push them out to the proper width; then the temple is locked into this position. When using a temple during weaving, it should be moved every couple of inches (4 or 5 cm).

Cutters

Various tools are available for cutting fabric into strips: manual scissors, electric scissors, rotary cutters, and specialty cutters from manufacturers such as Frazer and Rigby. No matter what type of cutting tool you use, it's very important to keep the blades sharpened for optimal cutting.

Manual scissors and rotary cutters are an inexpensive way to begin; later you can move to more expensive devices. Scissors are necessary for cutting irregularly shaped pieces of fabric and for numerous stripping methods. Invest in a pair of good-quality, sharp scissors that are comfortable in your hand. Rotary cutters are very efficient for making straight cuts. Look for ones that allow for a solid grip that provides good control. Because the replaceable circular blades of the rotary cutters are very sharp, they should always be used on a self-healing cutting mat.

For extensive cutting of heavy fabrics, such as canvas, corduroy, and denim, a Frazer or Rigby cutter is a wonderful tool. These cutters clamp onto a table and are adjustable so that you can vary the width of your strips. Though the initial investment may seem steep, their blades last a long time with proper care.

Another approach for cutting strips is to use a very sharp butcher's knife to slice through fabric that has been rolled very tightly. When using this method, continue rolling the fabric even after it has been initially rolled to make it tighten up nicely.

Alternatively, you can wet the rolled fabric and freeze it before slicing.

Fabric selvages from mill ends, still on the bolt, can be sliced with a band saw using a sharp, fine-tooth blade. Some mill end shops will slice to order.

Whenever you're cutting and weaving fabric strips, it is advisable to wear a dust mask.

Miscellaneous Tools

While designing and planning you will need:

- Journal or notebook

- Calculator

- Graph paper or point paper for working out ideas

- Stapler for attaching samples of the fabric to your notes for further reference

- 12-inch (30.5-cm) ruler to determine the sett and to do a quick warp wrapping

27

If you become involved with plied or twisted wefts, you will want an additional bobbin winder, spinning wheel, or the Schact Incredible Rope Machine.

For stripping and preparation of fabric, make sure you have these:

■ Dust mask

■ Sewing machine

■ Sewing thread

For winding warp and dressing the loom:

■ Masking tape

■ Heavy string for tying up lease sticks, etc.

These can come in handy while weaving:

■ T-pins for securing a broken warp thread as you are weaving

■ Bottle of liquid fray retardant to use for stabilizing the header or fringe

■ Large-eyed needles for darning any broken warp threads

■ Tape measure for many purposes, including measuring the length of your rug as it is woven

III

DESIGNING A RUG

Creativity begins with the individual. It is a marriage between human spirit and technical knowledge. Something as simple as plain weave has been used to create wonderful textiles all over the world by artists who dared to try something new with it. Breaking the cycle of assumptions and knowledge gained through formal training encourages personal creativity and exploration. The rugs presented in this book represent both traditional artists who gain inspiration from historical examples and maverick artists who are exploring new frontiers.

When designing your own rag rugs, it is important to understand and recognize what you like. Begin by developing a clear sense of what appeals to you. Purchase a sketchbook, a pen that you enjoy using, some colored pencils or markers, and a glue stick. Use the sketchbook to record your thoughts and ideas. Cut out images, patterns, and textures from magazines and other sources, and paste them into your sketchbook. Fill it with any images that strike your fancy—don't worry if they are good or not. The sketchbook is a place for observation, not judgment. Keep this journal handy, as you never know when ideas or images will occur; it will quickly grow into a valuable resource.

Colors, patterns, and designs are everywhere. Spend time looking closely at your surroundings— examining fabrics, books, and magazines, and visiting galleries, museums, botanical gardens, and zoos. When you see something that really catches your eye, take time to determine what about it excites or attracts you. What shapes, patterns, and textures do you see? Does it have rich dark tones, bright bold hues, or soft pale ones? Does it contain only a few colors or the whole spectrum? Is there a recognizable image, or is it abstract? Does it evoke a mood or feeling? Consider these questions seriously; by answering them and recognizing what moves you, you will get to know your personal aesthetic.

The world is full of wonderful inspirations, but don't forget to spend time looking inside yourself. This is a fertile space that is often neglected. Write down poems, phrases, or insights that pop into your head. Play word games with yourself. From time to time, let your mind wander and let your hand doodle whatever it wants. Getting to the point where you can allow answers and images to come from within takes some time to develop but is very rewarding.

As you come to understand your own taste in colors and design, you will slowly develop an individual style. Your style may not necessarily mesh with the color palette and trends of the interior design and fashion worlds. Don't let this concern you. If you love your design, you will enjoy the weaving process. Your rugs will be their strongest if they come from your creative soul and are a true reflection of you.

Once you have a firm understanding of your own creative language, you can allow space for flexibility and leeway when you're weaving a rug for someone else. With the acceptance and understanding of your own style, you won't simply be creating what they want; rather, you will incorporate their desires into your aesthetic "language."

In addition to functional and utilitarian associations—warmth, protection, cushioning—rugs can be viewed as eye-catching, dramatic, quiet, or harmo-nizing statements. A rug accessorizes a room, and depending on its look, it can add a bit of excitement or quiet elegance. In Western cultures the floor often gets overlooked or undervalued, but it is the foundation of any room. What you put on your floor is as important as what you put on your walls.

Take note of different floor coverings, regardless of their materials, and consider your response. How would you improve them? If you have never really thought about or looked at your relationship to the floor, begin to do so by laying pieces of fabrics down on the floor and noting your response, keeping in mind that fabric colors are often toned down a bit by the weaving process.

Color

One of the most important elements of designing a rug is color, and once you understand the basic principles of color, this sometimes frustrating

Orange inspirations for *Chessboard*, Heather Allen, 96" x 96" (244 x 244 cm), double bind, cotton warp with cotton, plastic bags, and plastic tape weft

PHOTO: EVAN BRACKEN

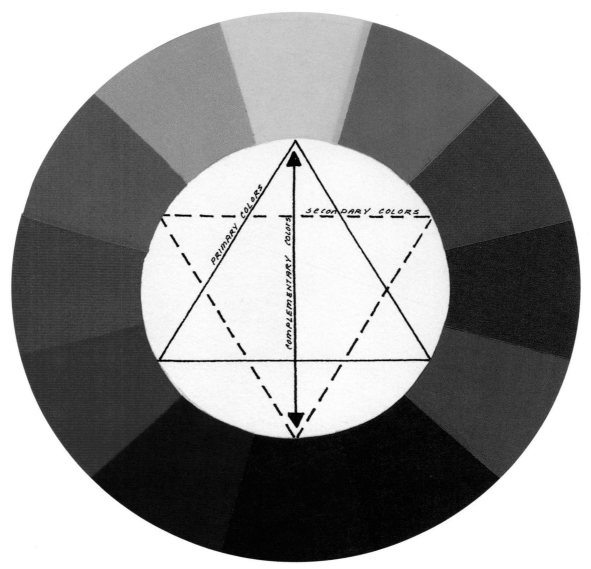

A fabric color wheel

design element loses its mystery. Learning about color is like any learning process—once you grasp it, it becomes intuitive.

Colors have four qualities by which they are defined: *hue, value, intensity,* and *temperature.* Hue is the basic quality by which we define a color; i.e., it is red, orange, yellow, green, blue, or purple. *Primary* colors are those that cannot be mixed: red, yellow, and blue. The *secondary* colors are those that result from mixing two primaries: orange (red plus yellow), green (blue plus yellow), and purple (blue plus red). *Complementary* colors are those opposite each other on the color wheel—red and green,

orange and blue, and yellow and purple. Complementary colors tend to electrify or intensify each other by creating high contrast. Depending on their relative values or intensities, they can also serve to balance each other. Colors next to each other on the color wheel—red and orange, blue and green, etc.—are called *analogous.* Because they share a common base (i.e., blue is in green), they blend well and create soothing, low-contrast palettes.

The value of a color is its lightness or darkness, which is based on the amount of black or white in it. It may take some time to train your eye to distinguish between the brightness of a color and its value. Squinting helps to reduce a color to its relative value. You can also use a value filter. These small acrylic filters cancel out hue and brightness and reduce fabrics to their light and dark values. This is helpful when planning a gradation or determining the value of a vibrant color.

The intensity of a color is its purity—how bright or dull it appears. In paints and dyes, a pure color can be made less intense by adding a small amount of its complement. Adding too much results in a gray or black color.

Using these three characteristics—hue, value, and intensity—we can determine that deep plum is a purple hue, possesses a dark value, and has a very low intensity. Similarly, fire-engine red is a red hue, possesses a medium value, and has a very high intensity.

The fourth characteristic, temperature, refers to how warm or cool a color appears. Colors containing a predominance of red or yellow are considered warm (think of fire and the warmth of the sun), and those containing blue (the cool ocean) are considered cool.

When thinking about colors for your rugs, remember that contrast can be based on color, value, intensity, and warmth or coolness. Cool colors, such as blues, greens, and purples, tend to recede and thus appear smaller; warm colors, such as reds, oranges, and yellows, advance and appear larger. This also holds true for value, with darker colors receding and lighter colors advancing.

Colored fabric is a little more complicated than flat color because it has dimensionality. As cloth is moved, folded, or compressed, color nuances appear because of the way the fabric absorbs and reflects light. These nuances will become a part of any rug you weave.

In addition to their basic qualities, colors are alive with distinct personalities. Two different combinations of the same colors can result in one composition that works together beautifully and another that fights horribly, depending on the placement and relationship of each color to the others. Colors are not islands. They are affected by and have an impact on neighboring colors and the warp. Depending on their color and value, rags will blend and harmonize or intensify and electrify.

Fabrics in the same color family but with different values and intensities

Because of the relationship of one color to its neighbor, richer and more complex colors may be achieved by creating a solid color area using various shades of a single hue. For example, if you want a red square or stripe in a Hit-and-Miss mixture, you might combine varying lengths of scarlet, maroon, straight red, dark red, orange-red, and vermilion. When woven into a rug, the overall color will be red, but the red will appear more vibrant than an area woven with a single colored fabric.

A good rule of thumb to follow when weaving a rag rug is to begin a bit brighter than you want the finished rug to be. Once the woven rug is on the floor, it won't be as close to you as it is on the loom, and the colors will appear more muted. Also, since textiles are organic and echo time, they will soften and mellow with age.

Because colors have individual personalities, the relationship between a person and any particular color is a very personal, emotional, and often highly intuitive one. When selecting a palette for your rug, let your eyes and heart, rather than your head tell you what to use. Choose colors that make you smile, colors that are gorgeous, alive, and exciting to you.

To find the colors and combinations you like best, continue working with your journal. Cut out pictures from magazines, collect postcards, snip fabric swatches, and find other examples of color combinations that appeal to you. After a while you will begin to see color trends or palettes in your collection of images. Spread out your rags and study them. Experiment by placing one on top of another. Now switch them around and watch as they appear to change color. Just as colors change in different environments, so will your response to them. By no means should you think of your palette as static.

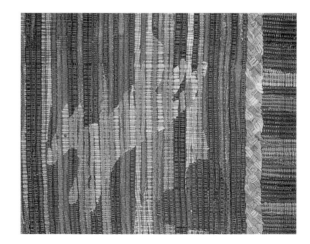

BELOW LEFT:
Quiescent Eucalypt, Sandra von Sneidern (Australian), 43½" x 85½" (110 x 217 cm), weft-faced plain weave and twill, linen warp with weft of cotton, linen, silk, and cotton/polyester blends
PHOTO SANDRA VON SNEIDERN:

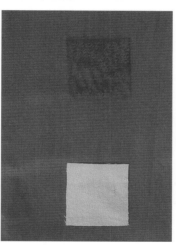
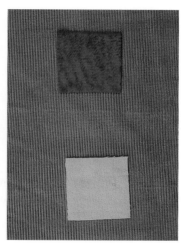

BELOW RIGHT:
Detail of *Quiescent Eucalypt*
PHOTO: SANDRA VON SNEIDERN

Composition

The final location and function of a rug are probably the most important considerations in its design. What room will the rug occupy, and what role will it play? Will it determine directional flow or traffic patterns? Will it serve as a room divider or a central focal point? Will it be a defining element in a formal dining room or a playful accent in a child's bedroom? Will it occupy a small space or fill an entire room? Must it turn a corner or climb a staircase?

In addition to its functional role, a rag rug can be viewed as an accessory that is eye catching and dramatic, or it can have a quiet, harmonizing presence. Due to the availability of an infinite variety of contemporary fabrics and a wide range of weaving styles, rag rugs can easily coordinate or match any interior design scheme. You can even weave a rug from the same upholstery fabric used for your draperies or sofa.

Once you determine the size and overall feeling of the rug, the next step is to decide what kind of surface texture you want it to have. Weaving is an interlocking grid composed of warp and weft elements. How these interact creates the surface texture of the rug. It is determined by both the weave structure and the sett or number of warp threads per inch.

The standard sett for rag rugs in the United States is 10 or 12 epi, which allows a weave where both

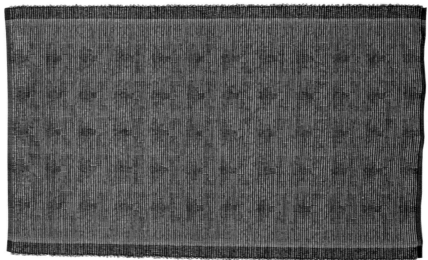

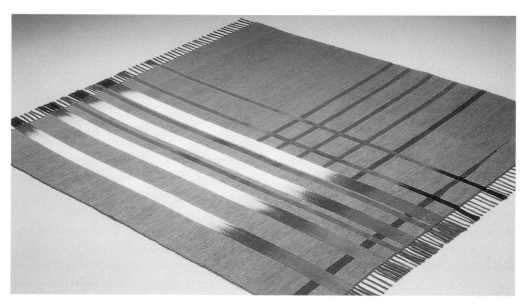

Figure 1

Warp compositions

the warp and weft are visible. This results in a synthesis of the warp and weft as they visually combine and create new colors.

Varying the sett across the rug is a nice way to create variety in the surface of the rug. A higher sett such as 15 or 16 epi produces a warp-dominant surface, and a sett of 5 or 6 allows the weft to completely obscure the warp. Since it is the warp that generally wears out first on a rag rug, the Scandinavian-style sett of 5 or 6 results in greater longevity. The design you choose will influence whether you want the warp to be an important element.

If you choose a sett that allows the warp to be visible, it can either be a subtle or a strong design element, depending on the warp pattern and colors you choose. As you are designing, consider that a light-colored warp will tend to dilute and mute weft colors; a warp having a medium value will tend to maintain the inherent integrity of weft colors; and a dark, intense, or vibrant warp will tend to enhance and intensify the colors of the weft. Think about balancing values (light, medium, and dark areas) within the rug.

Determining the warp is only the beginning step. The selection of weft rags plays a large part in how the warp will appear or disappear. If you weave multiple rugs on the same warp, you can make it very difficult to recognize their commonality simply by changing the design and weft colors.

There are many rag rug variations you can try, starting with simple plain weave and stripes. Stripes offer many interesting possibilities. Will your weft for each stripe be all one color or variegated? How

Figure 2
Weft compositions

broad will the stripes be? Will they be uniform or varied? The answers to these questions, combined with the colors you choose for each stripe and the relationship to each stripe to the other, can add many nuances to your finished piece. Scandinavians have a long tradition of utilizing the stripe motif with a simple warp. If you combine a striped warp with weft stripes, you will have plaid rugs similar to those woven by Scottish descendants in eastern Canada and northeastern United States.

Here are some other design ideas to consider:

- Solid-colored warp, leaving the design element to stripes, gradations, or Hit and Miss in the weft

- High-contrast stripes or blocks in light and dark or contrasting colors

- Salt-and-pepper or contrasting values or colors in the warp, alternating white–black–white or blue–orange–blue

- Asymmetrically striped warp in combination with a striped weft for dynamic plaids

- Gradual, soft transitions between colors or values in the warp and/or weft

- Juxtaposition of symmetrical and asymmetrical patterns

- A framing element 1 or 2 inches wide (2.5 or 5 cm) on either side of the rug, using the same color warp thread as for the weft of the header

- Hit and Miss with inlay accents

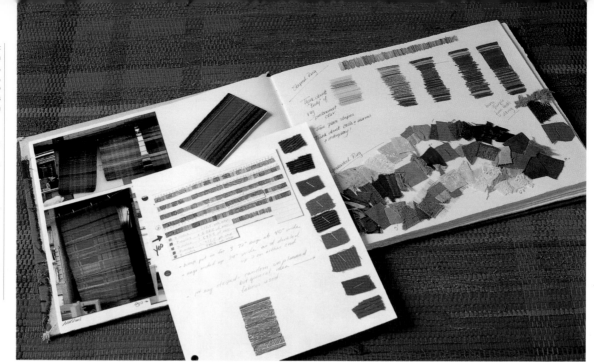

■ Twisted weft strips as accents or for larger areas

■ Proportions of the warp, weft, or both warp and weft based on the Fibonacci series. (Leonardo Fibonacci was a 13th century mathematician who developed a mathematical formula to create a series of proportions based on his studies of beautiful proportions found in nature. The sequence is 0, 1, 1, 2, 3, 5, 8,..., where each consecutive number is the sum of the two preceding numbers.)

Colored pencils and index cards are great tools for sketching design ideas. Use a small piece of card-

board for wrapping warp thread to get a visual test of your ideas. Remember to keep your sketches and your wrappings in the same proportions as the rug you intend to weave. Weaving is a partnership, a marriage between the warp and weft.

As you are designing your rug, have your weft fabric handy for visual reference and inspiration. You may find you need to supplement your colors or hand-dye some fabrics to achieve specific hues. Lay bundles of the colored rags on your work surface; then lay a couple of strands of the warp over different colors of the potential weft. What happens? Is it exciting or boring? Is the warp still visible or absorbed by the weft? Working directly with the fibers keeps you in touch with your materials.

It can be useful to cut snippets of the different fabrics and staple them to a piece of paper or alongside your sketch in the order that you plan to use them. Do keep in mind, though, that you may want to make additional changes and decisions at the loom once you begin weaving.

Many types of traditional rugs and carpets have borders. Though rag rugs often do not have formal borders, a border can act as a framing device that gives a rug the appearance of being a self-contained entity. Borders serve as boundaries and are there-

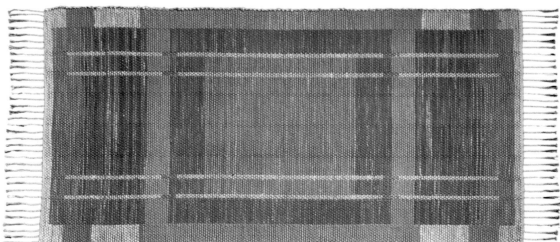

FAR LEFT:
Celestial Ponies,
**Missy Stevens
(American), 72"
x 72" (183 x 183
cm), inlay, mer-
cerized cotton
warp with cotton
corduroy weft
and braided ele-
ments**

LEFT, ABOVE:
*Asters in the
Grove—Zigzag,*
**Sara Hotchkiss
(American), 66"
x 60" (167.5 x
152.5 cm), tapes-
try technique,
Parisian cotton
warp and cotton
fabric weft**
PHOTO: DENNIS GRIGGS

LEFT, BELOW:
Sailing,
**Jutta Graf
(American), 44"
x 104" (112 x 264
cm), hand-dyed
cotton and linen
warp with cotton
and chenille rag
weft**
PHOTO: DARWIN
DAVIDSON

fore not appropriate to all designs. For example, a border on a long, striped rug would stifle its sense of rhythm, flow, and continuation. However in other cases, such as rugs that are more pictorial, they add a welcome sense of containment.

A border can be an integral part of the woven design of the rug, or it can be a separate finishing step done off the loom. The Shakers developed a style of rag rugs with braided borders, using narrow three-strand braids or heavier five- or seven-strand braids. Braids were used both singly and in multiples for a wider border.

As you create your designs, remember that there is no one weave structure that is the ideal for rag rugs. Rag thickness, color, and fiber content, together with the sett of the warp and its thickness and color are just some of the factors affecting your design. These many factors, plus weaving technique, produce a personal rug style unique to each weaver. Along your creative journey, there will be good rugs and okay rugs; not every rug will be your best, but you'll learn from each one. Keep in mind that your truly excellent rugs would not be possible if the earlier ones had not helped to inform and educate you.

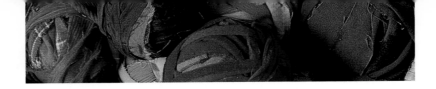

IV

PREPARING THE WEFT, WARPING & WEAVING

I met an aged man

I asked him

"What is the time?"

"Time," he replied,

"Is the warp of life.

Tell the young, the gay

To weave it well."

THANKFUL BARRON TAYLOR 1801-1896

Weft Preparation

BELOW:
Rag strips in color bundles

Once you've established your design, it's time to prepare the weft strips. This is also the time to obtain any missing colors because once you start weaving, you won't want to stop and go looking for them. All your fabric and rags should be washed

and dried before using. If you're working with clothing, begin by taking off all the buttons, zippers, seams, and pockets. Save the seams, especially from heavier clothes, to tie rolled-up rag pieces and strips into neat color bundles. These bundles are a good way to keep your fabrics organized.

Both stripping rags and weaving create a fair amount of dust. A dust mask should always be worn while stripping and can also be worn while weaving. It's a good idea to vacuum frequently so that the dust doesn't accumulate or travel to other areas.

Generally fabric is cut into strips ½ inch (1.5 cm) wide for heavier cloth, such as denim and corduroy, 1 to 1½ inch (2.5 to 4 cm) wide for most regular fabrics, and 2 to 4 inches (5 to 10 cm) wide for lightweight plastics and silks. Since the intent is to have the weft shots fairly similar in packed thickness regardless of the fabric, you may need to strip fabrics for the same rug into a variety of widths. This may mean that a silk blouse is cut into strips

Selection of rag rugs drying on a clothesline, Judi Gunter (Canadian), cotton warp and wool weft
PHOTO: JUDI GUNTER

4 inches (10 cm) wide and a chenille bathrobe is cut into ½-inch (1.5-cm) strips. Ultimately they will both twist down to the same pencil thickness.

If you plan to weave a gradation or use another technique with two or more wefts per shot, the width of each weft strip should be narrower. A good test is to cut a sample of the each weft fabric and twist the pieces together; the combination should be roughly equal in diameter to a standard lead pencil. Adjust the width of your strips to achieve this even thickness.

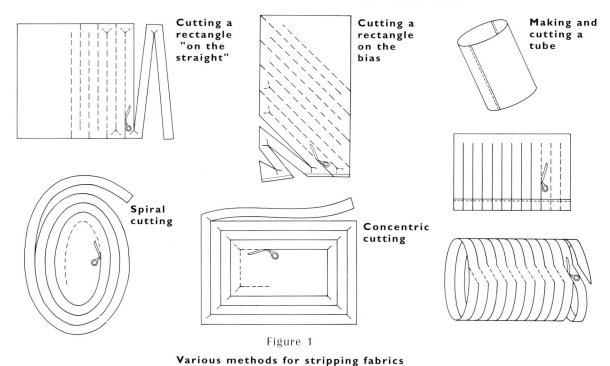

Cutting a rectangle "on the straight"

Cutting a rectangle on the bias

Making and cutting a tube

Spiral cutting

Concentric cutting

Figure 1

Various methods for stripping fabrics

Rag weft sewn into a continuous strip, ready for cutting

These include strip width, warp sett, how tightly you pack the weave (picks per inch/centimeter), size of rug, and rug thickness. Lightweight weaves require less fabric than double-faced weaves.

It is always best to weave a test sample to determine how many picks you are getting per inch (centimeter) of weaving. Once you have that information, you can estimate the total length of a particular rag strip using this model (substitute centimeters for inches if you use metric measurements): If there are 6 picks per inch and 6 total inches of that color in the design (3 inches at each end of the rug) then you will need 6 x 6 = 36 picks. If the width of the rug including draw-in is 26.4 inches (24 + 2.4 inches draw-in), then you will need at least 26.4 x 36 = 950.4 inches of that color strip.

You should always be generous with these calculations and keep in mind that switching colors takes up extra weft. It is difficult to translate total weft length when looking at a garment, but good record keeping and experience over time will increase your knowledge of the amounts you can expect. It is always good to have some extra colors on hand to add at the last minute if necessary.

As a rule, begin with at least 4 to 5 pounds (1.8 to 2.3 kilos) for your first rug. Weigh your fabric before you start weaving and subtract any leftovers at the end. Keep records of how much fabric you use, the sett of the warp, and the finished size of the rug. You will soon develop an intuition for how much fabric you will need to weave a rug.

It's a good idea to dress the loom before stripping your rags so that you can do small weaving tests to evaluate and adjust the width of your rag strips. Cut different widths of the fabrics you plan to use and test-weave them. They should pack firmly and create the desired thickness. Once you've found a width that creates the desired results, use it as a guide. In time you will come to know how wide to cut your strips and the need for testing will diminish.

Rag strips can be ripped or cut with scissors or rotary cutters. Although ripping is often faster, it produces more dust and frayed edges. Extensive ripping is best done with slightly damp cloth, as it rips more easily and creates less dust. There are a number of cutters available (see page 26), and your choice depends on what best suits your needs. As you finish stripping each garment, tie the strips together to keep them orderly.

If you prepare weft strips in assembly-line fashion, it won't seem as large a job. When friends come over, ask them to pitch in and help. You can combine visiting with your weft preparation.

HOW MUCH FABRIC WILL YOU NEED?

There are many variables involved in determining the amount of fabric required to weave a rag rug.

JOINING THE STRIPS

Once all the fabric is in strips, there are various ways to join them. Some people leave the rag strips unsewn and simply lay them in by hand, but I prefer to sew them together. I slightly overlap the ends and sew the strips into a long rope, using a tight straight stitch or zigzag. If you sew the strips together as shown in figure 3, you will create a continuous strip of loops that needs snipping only between the seams. Heavier fabrics, such as denim, can be sewn on a diagonal and trimmed to reduce the bulkiness of the joint.

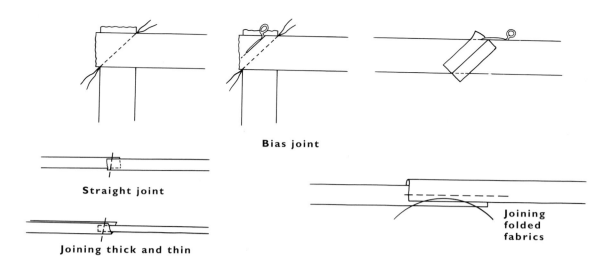

Bias joint

Straight joint

Joining thick and thin

Joining folded fabrics

Figure 2

Joining the strips

There are also various looping techniques for joining strips without sewing. Some of these have colorful local names such as "slit and loop" and "skin the cat." Using fabric glue is yet another method of joining.

All the strips from a single fabric can be sewn together, or you can create Hit-and-Miss ropes. A traditional Hit-and-Miss pattern means that you randomly sew strips together, paying little attention to their order. A rug woven of this weft will be a total surprise. You can also use this technique within a block of color to give it added depth and richness.

Traditionally once the rags were joined, they were wound into balls and stored. Another alternative is to keep them tied in bundles ready for weaving.

Warping

The instructions included here are for making a chain warp and warping the loom from back to front. There are other methods you can use, such as warping on from front to back, and many production rag rug weavers do sectional warping that allows them to wind warps that are from 50 to 90 yards (45.7 to 82.3 m) long. In the case of sectional warping, the small segments of the warp are wound directly from the spools onto a sectional warp beam on the loom.

Figure 3

Sewing a continuous strip

Rag weft wound into balls

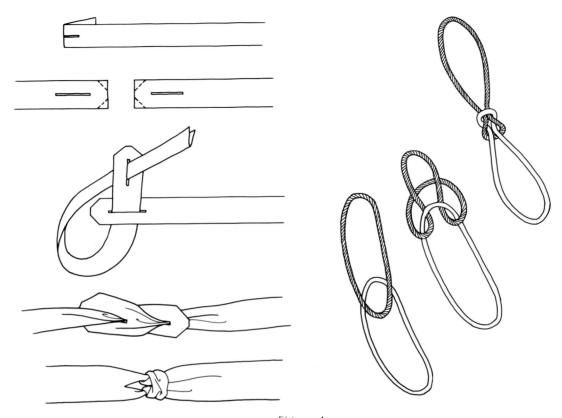

Figure 4

Nonsewn joining techniques

WARP CALCULATIONS

Once you have determined the sett and warp pattern of the rug, you are ready to begin your warp calculations. It is a good idea to keep records of the warps you wind, including all calculations. When calculating the length of your warp, there are two important factors to consider. The first is *take-up*—the amount of warp that is consumed by the weaving process—and the other is *loom waste*—the warp that is necessary for tying on to the loom but is unweavable. The take-up percentage increases when wider strips or stiffer rags are used for the weft.

Calculating 6 inches (15 cm) for a fringe allowance is standard, but the amount may vary depending on the edging treatments. Plied, braided, or knotted fringe takes up more warp than simple overhand knots.

Here are the calculations necessary for determining the length of each warp thread. The example is for a rug 24 by 36 inches, but you can substitute any dimensions in inches or centimeters.

LENGTH OF RUG	36
TAKE-UP: 20% OF LENGTH (36 × .2)	+ 7
FRINGE (6 inches per end)	+12
LOOM WASTE (varies according to loom)	+36
TOTAL WARP LENGTH	91 inches or 3 yards

(always round up to the next full yard)

To calculate the number of warp threads across the rug, you must first estimate the amount of *draw-in* that occurs in your weaving. Draw-in is the pulling in of the width of the rug as it is woven. Large amounts of draw-in are generally caused by weft that is laid in too tightly; using a temple can help prevent excessive draw-in.

The amount of take-up and draw-in that occur will depend on the weaver, the weave structure, the material, and width of the weft. The calculations shown here are to serve only as guidelines. As you keep notes of your rugs, the materials used, their on-loom and off-loom dimensions, and the weave structures, you will begin to note differences in these two factors and can adjust your calculations accordingly.

This is the calculation for the number of warp threads needed for our sample rug:

RUG WIDTH	24
DRAW-IN: 10% OF WIDTH (.1 x 24)	+ 2.4
	26.4
MULTIPLIED BY THE EPI (in this case 10)	x 10
TOTAL NUMBER OF WARP THREADS	264

Draw-in increases when you use thinner rags or knitted fabrics for your weft. It decreases to almost zero when wide strips of stiff fabric, such as heavy denim, are used.

The total yards of warp needed for a rug 24 by 36 inches is 264 ends x 3 yards = 792 yards. One cone of carpet warp would probably be sufficient for a rug this size if you plan to use a solid-colored warp. Since it's more exciting to weave on a multicolored warp, you may want to purchase several colors and use fractions of each. Keep track of approximately how much warp you remove from each cone so that you know how much remains for another project. (Hint: If you want to conserve warp, wind on more than one rug at a time. No matter how long you make the warp, loom waste remains constant.)

WINDING THE WARP

Divide the total number of warp ends into sections that can be manageably wound onto the pegs of the warping frame. You don't want threads overlapping or falling off. For a 24-inch (61-cm) rug, divide the warp in half, into two 12-inch (30.5-cm) sections that will be wound separately.

Measure a guide string that is the same length as the warp, but of a distinctly contrasting color. Determine the best configuration of the guide string on the warping frame or reel, and put a piece of masking tape on the board above the warp cross, marking the tape with arrows to indicate the crossing directions.

Place your warp cones on cone holders or in buckets on the floor so that the warp will unwind freely as you pull it. Using heavy string that contrasts in color with the warp palette, cut numerous 12-inch (30.5-cm) ties.

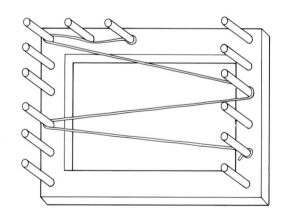

Figure 5
Placing the guide string

Figure 6
Direction at the cross

Tie the warp string onto the warping frame with a loop that fits freely over the top peg. Then follow the guide string to wind the warp onto the frame. If any knots appear in the warp as it comes off the cone, cut and retie the thread so that all knots are at either end of the warp and not in the middle. When you change colors, always tie on at either end and not in the middle. As you wind the warp, concentrate on keeping the tension even.

If you need to take a break in the midst of winding the warp, simply loop the thread a couple of times over one of the pegs. This will hold the warp at an even tension and allow you to commence again without any inconvenience.

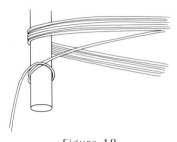

Figure 10

Looping the thread

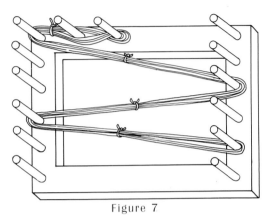

Figure 7

Warp on the frame

Using one of your 12-inch (30.5-cm) ties, group the warp threads in 1-inch (2.5-cm) increments at the cross (fig. 8). After you've wound a complete section, (in this example 12 inches/30.5 cm), place very tight choke ties every yard or so. Tie loose ties on the top and bottom of both sides of the warp cross and at both warp ends (fig. 9).

Beginning at the bottom of the frame, gently remove the warp and begin looping it upon itself, using your hands as though you were crocheting. Keep the warp loose and continue to chain up to the cross. Repeat this process for each section, labeling their order, and lay them in the correct order on your work surface or loom bench.

Figure 8

Ties at the cross

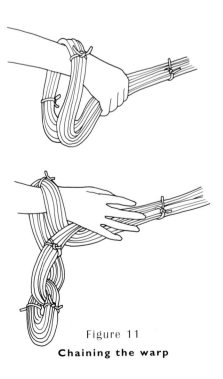

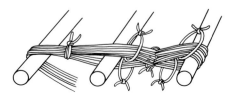

Figure 9

Choke and loose ties

Figure 11

Chaining the warp

BEAMING ON THE WARP

The first step in beaming on the warp is to prepare the loom. Center and secure the raddle to the back beam. Masking tape or a heavy rubber band works well for this, or you can tie it securely with heavy string. Count the heddles to make sure there are enough on each shaft; then push them to the left side.

With the cross end of the warp over the back beam, lay the warp through the open shafts, over the beater, and across the front beam. Insert the lease sticks, placing one on either side of the warp cross. To facilitate separating the cross, grasp the cross ties and pull gently. Then tie the ends of the lease sticks together, using a square knot to provide a slight separation between the two. Using a long piece of string at each end of the lease sticks, suspend them between the castle and the back beam.

Starting with one half, evenly distribute the warp across the raddle, working from the center toward the side. Repeat with the other half. Make sure that the warp sections are attached in the correct sequence and that the threads don't become twisted. Place large rubber bands over the nails of the raddle to keep the warp from slipping out.

Detach the separate bar from the warp beam apron, thread it through the uncut warp ends, and reattach it to the apron.

As you wind the warp onto the warp beam, place thin cardboard, sticks, or large sheets of paper between the layers of the warp. (A continuous length of paper or flexible cardboard works most easily.) This prevents the outer layers of thread from slipping down between the inner ones and creating uneven tension.

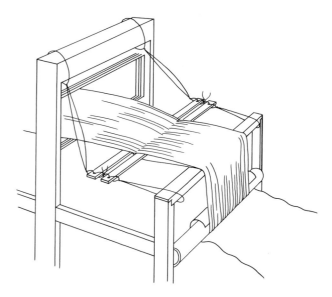

Figure 13
Separating the warp with paper or cardboard

The warp should be held from the front of the loom, in even tension, as it is wound. A relatively narrow warp can be divided into small groups and temporarily looped onto the front beam to hold it taut. For a wider warp, an assistant or two can be helpful. Have one person divide the warp in half and grasp it firmly as you would hold the reins of a horse, untying the choke ties as necessary. Plucking the warp threads like guitar strings or shaking them can help straighten out any tangled or snarled areas. The second person can begin slowly to wind on the warp.

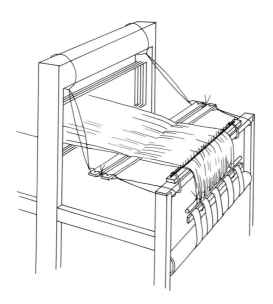

Figure 12
Beaming on the warp with lease sticks and raddle in place

Sunshine from the Deep Sea, Chiyoko Kumon (Japanese), 55" x 94½" (140 x 240 cm), cotton thread warp with strips of 60-100 year old indigo-dyed cotton clothes and futon covers
PHOTO: HIDEAKI MIYAKE

Make sure the packing material—i.e., the cardboard or sticks—is sufficiently wide enough so that the warp winds on evenly and does not overlap, form a barrel shape, or fall off the ends of the separating material. Any of these occurrences will cause uneven tension in your warp and ultimately affect the finished rug. Once the rug is off the loom and lying in a relaxed state on the floor, uneven tension will become apparent.

Wind on until the end of the warp is inside the front beam.

At this point, the raddle is no longer necessary and can be removed. Cut the ends of the warp and tie them in a slip knot or noose knot to hold them temporarily while threading the heddles.

Figure 14
Winding on the warp

Figure 15
Slip knot

Reading a Draft

In order to thread the heddles, you first must know which warp threads should be attached to which shafts. Drafts are schematic diagrams that provide the necessary information not only for threading, but also for tie-up and treadling for a specific weave structure. Drafts are written in an international language, with slight variations among weavers. They are simple and straightforward once you become familiar with them.

THREADING DRAFT

The order in which the warp is threaded through the heddles of the loom is called the *draw*. A threading draft is generally drawn on graph paper, which echoes the inherent grid of most woven textiles. It is read from bottom to top, mirroring the order in which the heddles occur from front to back on the loom. An X is generally used to indicate which shaft holds the heddle.

A quick look at the threading draft will tell you how many shafts are necessary to weave any rug. The project rugs in chapter 7 of this book require from two to eight shafts.

Floating selvages, which are threaded through the reed but not threaded through the heddles, are generally double-sleyed and denoted by an O.

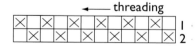

Figure 16

Threading draft for two shafts

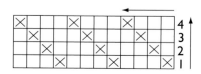

Figure 17

Threading draft for four shafts

TIE-UP DRAFT

Generally positioned to the immediate right of the threading draft, a tie-up draft indicates which shafts are to be lifted independently or simultaneously to create a shed. It is read from left to right for the treadle sequence and from bottom to top for the shafts. An O indicates the treadle and the shaft to which it is tied. Each loom has a system for tying up the treadles to one or more shafts, depending on the weave pattern requirements.

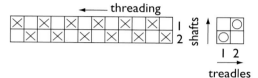

Figure 18

Tie-up draft for two shafts

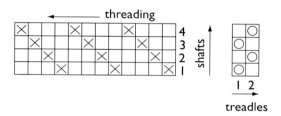

Figure 19

Tie-up draft for four shafts

TREADLING DRAFT

Located just above the tie-up draft, the treadling draft indicates the sequence for depressing the treadles to create the sheds necessary for the desired pattern. It is generally read from bottom to top.

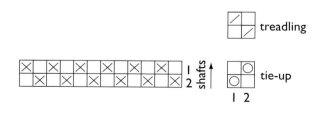

Figure 20

Treadling draft for two shafts (plain weave)

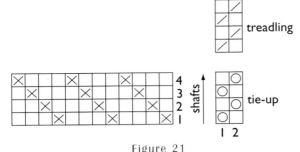

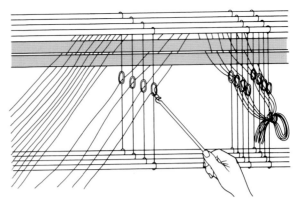

Figure 21

Treadling draft for four shafts (plain weave)

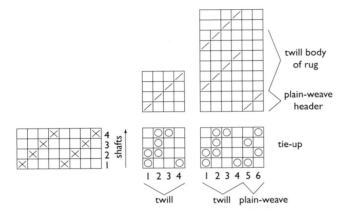

Figure 22

Treadling draft for four shafts (twill with plain-weave header)

Dressing the Loom

With your threading draft in hand, now it is time to dress the loom. These instructions describe the method for plain weave (tabby), but with minor variations, it can used for any weave structure.

Starting at the right and moving slowly to the left, draw each thread through a heddle using a heddle or threading hook. Because the lease sticks are still in place, you should be able to take the threads in order from the cross area and thread them through the heddles.

Begin threading the heddles, alternating 1, 2, 1, 2 with a two-shaft loom or 1, 2, 3, 4, 1, 2, 3, 4 for four shafts. Work in small groups of eight, double check the threading, and secure the threaded ends with a slip knot or noose knot.

Center the reed within the beater and mark the

Figure 23

Threading the heddles

center of the reed. Measure half the width of the rug and mark that point to the right of the center mark. The second mark indicates where to begin sleying.

How the reed is sleyed depends upon its relationship to the sett of the warp. Using the example of a rug woven at 10 epi, a #10 reed allows you to have one thread per dent. With a #20 reed, you would need to skip every other dent, and a #5 reed would require two threads per dent. In general, it's best to distribute the warp threads evenly.

Starting from the right, sley the reed accordingly and secure the warp ends in small groups with an overhand knot on each. You can also sley from the middle to each side. Take care that no warp threads cross or twist between the heddles and the reed.

Once the reed has been fully sleyed and the threading checked once more, untie and remove the lease sticks.

Gather the warp threads into groups 1 or 2 inches (2.5 or 5 cm) thick—or in bunches of 10 or 20 threads for our 10 epi example. Starting with the group in the center, tie the warp threads onto the cloth beam apron bar with half knots, alternating groups on either side of the center. Once the warp is completely tied on, begin again in the center and tighten and secure each knot, checking to make sure that the tension is even across the entire

52

warp. Patting the warp lightly with an open palm is a good way to check the tension. Linen and some seine twine warps have no "give" and must be carefully adjusted and retied until the tension is even all the way across.

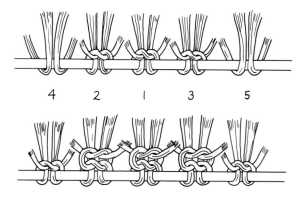

Figure 24

Tying on to the apron bar

Tie up your treadles for the two sheds necessary for plain weave. With a two-shaft loom, one shaft is attached to each treadle. If you are using a four shafts, then shafts 1 and 3 are attached to one treadle and shafts 2 and 4 are attached to the other. Now you are ready to weave!

Weaving the Rug

Begin weaving with filler; two shots in each shed will allow easy removal later. Continue weaving until the warp threads are evenly spaced across the weft. If you want a fringed header, continue weaving about 6 inches (15 cm) of filler before beginning the header.

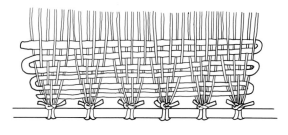

Figure 25

Filler

The header is woven using warp-weight thread or rags that are thinner than your weft. It ensures that the weft is held in place when the rug is removed from the loom. Doubled or tripled warp thread makes a nice header and creates a rolled hem that is similar in thickness to the body of the rug. I generally use a hemmed edging, so I weave a 1½- to 2-inch (4- to 5-cm) header using two threads of warp, generally of different colors. If you are planning a fringe or tied finishing, weave a ½- to 1-inch (1.5- to 2.5-cm) header. Weave 1 to 2 inches (2.5 to 5 cm) if you want a rolled sewn hem. (See chapter 6 for various finishing techniques.) If in doubt, weave more rather than less, as it is easy to take out extra weft but nearly impossible to add it.

Weaving the filler and header

Now you are ready to weave the body of your rug. Place the prepared weft strips on a work surface in the sequence in which they will be woven. If you're planning a symmetrical design, divide the rags in half. This will let you know if you are running short and need to supplement any colors.

Load a ski shuttle by placing a slip knot over the shuttle prong and wrapping the rags until the shuttle is full. When using a rag shuttle, tie a weft end around one of the bars and wrap it until it's full. You can prepare numerous shuttles at a time or wind them as you go.

Creating a weaver's angle on each shot and placing the temple

Lay in your first weft strip, leaving a 3- to 4-inch (7.5- to 10-cm) tail with the loose end. The first strip you lay in is the most important, as it sets the tone for the rest of the rug. It also has two selvages for you to prepare.

Begin with the tail. Change the shed and beat the first weft strip into place. Now twist the tail firmly toward the warp, adjust the edge so that it looks neat, and use your index finger to pack the twisted weft into the next row. It will be held there by the next pass of the weft.

At the other side, pass the shuttle back through the shed, creating a weaver's angle or bubble in your weft. A weaver's angle provides the amount of fabric necessary to allow for the weft to travel up and down across the warp, without causing the selvages to pull inward. As you continue weaving successive rows, create a weaver's angle with each pass of the shuttle before beating. This will give you uniform, tight selvages and reduce draw-in. Using a temple (see page 26) can also help prevent draw-in.

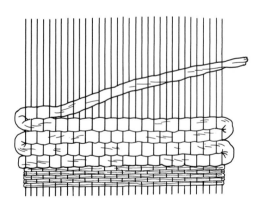

Figure 26

Weaver's angle

If you choose not to sew your strips together, the ends should tapered. Overlap the strips 3 inches (7.5 cm), change the shed, and beat. The ends will stay in place within the body of the rug. Care should be taken so that the overlaps do not fall near the selvages.

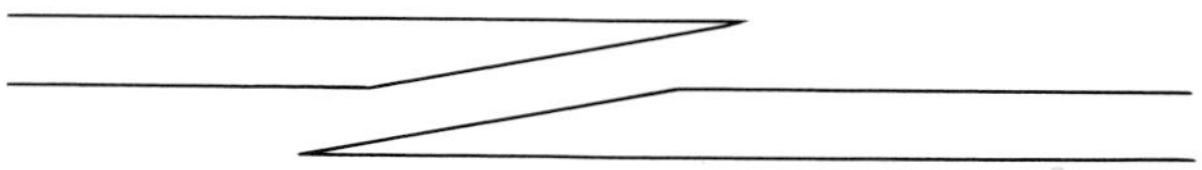

Figure 27

Tapering the ends of the weft

A good rag rug should be tightly packed. This does not necessarily mean that one should beat hard, but that each pull of the beater should be a firm pull and involve the weight of the weaver rather than just the upper arm muscles. If beating is difficult for you, consider using a weighted beater to help you achieve a firmly packed rug.

As you are weaving, it's necessary to keep track of the length of your rug as it is rolled onto the cloth beam. A tape measure or measuring string pinned along one side works fine. I use measuring strings tied in loops through the selvage at 1-foot (30.5-cm) intervals to make counting easy. On these strings, you can add pieces of masking tape with measurements.

Weave the desired length for the body of your rug, moving the temple every couple of inches (about every 5 cm). Remember to calculate and add the take-up to the length of the rug.

After you have finished weaving the body of the rug, weave a header using the same doubled warp thread or thin rags that you used at the beginning. You can use the same colors or contrasting colors. The header can be a separate design element or a continuation of the design of the rug body.

Once the weaving is done, release the brake and cut the rug from the loom, allowing sufficient extra warp for the fringe or other finishing method.

V

VARIATIONS IN WEFT, WEAVE & DESIGN

Finnish Stripes,
**Wynne Mattila (American), 36"
x 66" (91.5 x
167.5 cm), 15-
ply Finnish
seine twine
warp and cot-
ton fabric weft**
PHOTO: CHRISTINE
BENKERT

The creative potential of rag rugs is endless. Time and time again throughout my research, I have been excited and inspired by photographs or slides of yet more wonderful rag rugs from weavers all over the world. This chapter introduces a medley of simple and complex ideas and weave structures. Peruse these pages and dream about your own rug designs, keeping in mind that creativity is synonymous with experimentation and courage.

Weft & Warp Variations

▼

STRIPES

Historically rag rugs were often woven in patterns characteristic of different areas or ethnic origins, such as the striped rugs generally associated with Scandinavia and the tartan plaids woven by Scottish Americans.

Stripes are natural motifs for rag rugs—wonderful, simple, and timeless designs. Stripes appear in textile designs, both historic and contemporary, from cultures all over the world. Thick or thin, balanced or unbalanced, combined with a neutral warp, or paired with a strong striped warp to create a plaid, the possibilities for striped patterns are endless. You may not need to go any further. Stripes in themselves are enough to occupy a lifetime of exploration.

When designing with stripes, think of the overall impact you would like to create—bold and brassy, with a strong color or value contrast, or delicate and subtle, created by softer hues and a low-value contrast.

Wynne Mattila has traveled to Finland, where she encountered numerous striped rag runners. This experience reconnected her with her "stripe gene," and she feels more certain than ever of her preference for striped designs. Do you have a stripe gene?

A very subtle striped rug can be woven using a traditional Finnish shuttle technique whereby two or three shuttles are loaded with different colored wefts. These are woven in a repeating order to create a very dense rug with fine stripes. This same technique can used to make color gradations. (See Wynne's project in chapter 7.)

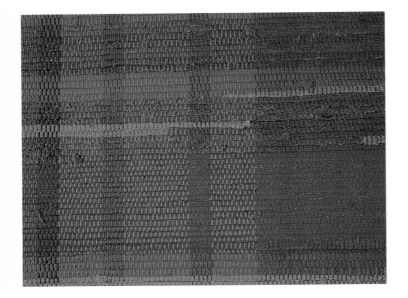

PLAIDS

What do you get when you have stripes in the weft and stripes in the warp? A wonderful plaid! If you have any Scottish blood in your family, you may have a book on tartans that offers endless design variations. You could use these patterns to make your family tartan for a surprise gift.

Plaids can be complex and detailed or simple and large. Varying weft colors or introducing gradations can produce interesting and unique plaid rugs. Like stripes, plaids can be dramatic due to color or value contrast, or they can be subtle and quiet. A balanced plaid is created by weaving the same succession of colors in the weft as in the warp.

GRADATIONS

In contrast to the graphic quality often associated with striped and plaid motifs, gentle color or value gradations are a wonderful way to create airy or atmospheric effects with rag rugs. Simple gradations, which use two or three shuttles, can create gradual painterly blending of colors. When planning a gradation, it can be helpful to lay out your fabrics and arrange them in weaving order until they make a gradual progression of color, value, or color and value.

There are a number of ways to achieve a gradation in weaving. The simplest gradation uses only one shuttle, and it is accomplished at the sewing machine when the strips are sewn together. Begin with one color, and as that color ends, alternate strips of the next color with those of the first color. Then sew strips of just the second color until you are ready to add the third. Continue this process for the remainder of the rug.

Another, smoother gradation technique involves using two shuttles wound with thin strips of separate colors. Two thin weft strips are woven in each shed. Begin by weaving with color A and color B for the desired width; then drop color A and pick up color C. Weave with colors B and C for the desired width; then drop color B and pick up color D. Continue in the same manner for the rest of

TOP:
Plaid Rug #1,
Heather Allen,
48" x 72" (122 x
183 cm),
plain weave,
cotton/polyester
warp and weft
PHOTO: EVAN BRACKEN

ABOVE:
Rug #37,
Chad Alice
Hagen
(American), 38"
x 74" (96.5 x
188 cm), cor-
duroy weft in
color gradation
on striped cot-
ton warp
PHOTO: NELL YTSMA

Although stripes can be beautiful when created in simple plain weave, more complex weave structures add interesting surface textures. Mary Ann Wise's *Rug #2* is a peaceful array of stripes that looks even richer once you become aware of the complex surface created by the weft-faced bound weave. This type of rug has a strong visual impact from a distance and an added surface interest when you get closer to it. Her subtle palette results from careful color manipulation. For her weft, Mary Ann dyes recycled cotton bed sheets by hand.

the rug. You can add more interest by interjecting a random stripe or stripes of color that don't appear anyplace else in the rug. Although this approach tends to use a large number of colors, the richness of the surface is well worth the effort. Chad Alice Hagen is a master of this technique, as seen in her corduroy rug.

HIT AND MISS

Historically rag rug weaving was a social practice, and there were rag sewing bees, similar to the more well-known quilting bees. At those events, people gathered to prepare, strip, and join rags together. The expression *Hit and Miss* evolved from this earlier period, when rags were collected and saved, sorted, stripped, randomly sewn, balled, and taken to the local weaver to be made into rugs. The weaver had no choice but to weave the strips in the order in which they were sewn.

A slightly more formal version is the planned Hit and Miss, also called a tube rug. The effect lies somewhere between gradations and striped designs. It is a very simple yet effective way to create a strong repeat design that is nonlinear. The weft fabric, generally an assortment of five colors, is sewn into a tube and cut. A repeating diamond pattern appears in the woven rug due to the regularity of the spacing and length of the colored rag strips. Debra Sharpee combines this with warp striping to create very interesting and colorful rugs. (See her project in chapter 7.)

TWISTED WEFT PATTERNS

Rhythm and directional designs can be created within individual passes of the weft by twisting or plying two rag strips of contrasting colors. When two shots of twisted wefts are used, one an S-twist and one a Z-twist, the pattern is often referred to as *herringbone, arrow pattern, turkey tracks, barber pole, flock of geese,* or *Shaker-style twisted wefts.*

Twisting wefts is very simple and follows the same principle as plying two strands together. If you want just a couple of twisted shots for design emphasis, they can be twisted at the loom while the two weft

LEFT;
Beached,
Sandra von Sneidern (Australian), 43½" x 71" (110 x 180 cm), plain weave with twill inlay, 8/4 linen warp, cotton and cotton/polyester weft
PHOTO: SANDRA VON SNEIDERN

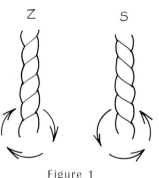

Figure 1
Z-twist and S-twist

shots are in the same shed. Twisting short lengths at the loom allows you to control the twist direction. Use two thinner wefts either of contrasting value, such as black and white, or of contrasting color, such as magenta and turquoise. The stronger the contrast between the colors of the twisted strips, the more graphic the pattern will be. Twisted wefts are often used in combination with solid-colored areas to highlight the twist pattern.

Turkey tracks or herringbone patterns are common weaving designs seen in the textiles of many cultures. In the U.S., the Shakers were well known for their use of twisted wefts in their rugs. They generally alternated a couple of shots of the twisted rag wefts with areas of solid-colored, wool yarn. Twisted wefts are a nice way to create an accent of color or pattern. Margaret Shaw weaves rugs in the Shaker tradition, using a combination of twisted yarn and rag strips.

If you want large quantities of twisted wefts, you can use a spinning wheel, the Incredible Rope Machine from Schact Company, or two hand-cranked bobbin winders. If you use hand-cranked bobbin winders, you will also need a number of extra-large elastic bands cut once to make long ties. The ties are used to hold the rag "rope" onto the winder. The basic idea is first to twist the rags

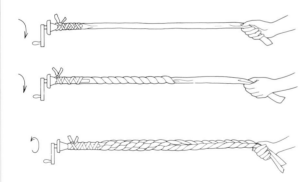

Figure 2
Twisting weft on bobbin winders

fairly tightly in one direction, then twist the two together on one bobbin winder in the reverse direction. The other end of the rag strips can be fastened to a chair, but having someone hold them for you makes the job quicker and more fun. By varying the twisting directions, you can make weft that is twisted in either S- or Z-patterns. For a random twill pattern, try twisting strips of cloth that have been sewn Hit and Miss.

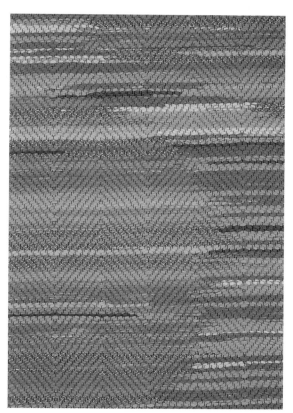

Two-color twisting is an effective way to create an image or surface design effect without using a more complicated weave structure. It is a simple technique, yet it can be very sophisticated, as seen in Ingela Norén's striking example, *River*. Within each color, she uses various shades to make the rug richer and more vibrant. In *River*, Ingela has also used a twill weave structure to add interest to the surface.

Two-color twisting is achieved by winding two different color strips around the same shuttle so that one is stacked on top on the other. When shot

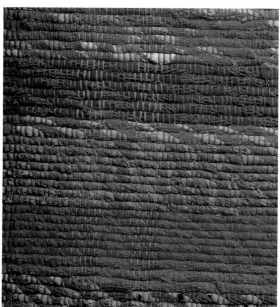

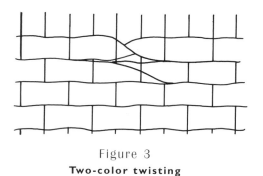

Figure 3
Two-color twisting

Detail of
Il Faut,
Catherine K
(Australian/
French), full
size is 18½" x
118" (47 x 300
cm), meet-and-
separate tapes-
try technique,
cotton warp
and newsprint
weft
PHOTO: CATHERINE K

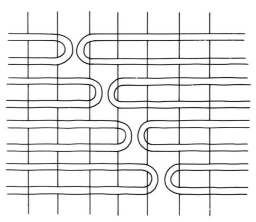

Meet and separate

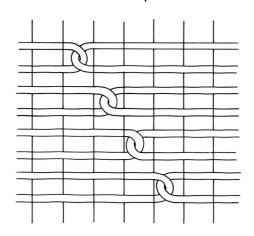

Clasped weft

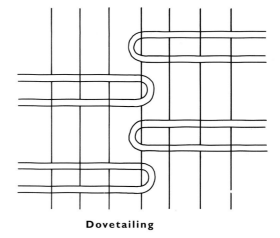

Dovetailing

Figure 4
Tapestry techniques

through the shed, the individual strips are manipulated by hand so that one color dominates and the other is mostly hidden. After twisting the strips, change the shed to hold them in place, then beat. The overall effect is one-sided, due to the fact that the weft manipulation is being done from the top. It is difficult to see what is happening on the other face of the rug, and thus a spontaneous design results. The edges and nuances, the peeking out of the repressed color, create a strong image without the hard edges of many loom-controlled designs.

TAPESTRY

Tapestry is an ancient weaving technique that lends itself to traditional uses as well as contemporary designs. In tapestry, the weft is manipulated by hand to create geometric, landscape, and other image-oriented designs. It is much like drawing with cloth. Basic tapestry techniques are very simple and yet allow a weaver the freedom to create innumerable designs as they weave. Since it is through weft manipulation that the designs are created, plain weave may be used for the underlying structure of the rug.

There are three basic tapestry techniques: *meet and separate, clasped weft,* and *dovetailing.* In meet and separate, the weft strips come together without interlocking with each other or with a common warp thread. As a result, tiny slits are formed where the two wefts meet. (This technique is also called *slit tapestry.*) When using meet and separate

for rugs, the slits should be sewn shut by hand to improve their wearability for floor use. In the clasped weft technique, the two colors of weft

come together and interlock before turning back in the next shed. Dovetailing results when two wefts interlock a common warp thread on alternate shots.

A strong communal rag rug tradition exits in the mountainous areas of Slovakia, where weavers often use tapestry techniques for making rag rugs both for the floor and for wall hangings. The region is still largely agrarian, and the rag rugs are woven during the winter months, when the looms are brought inside and set up. In their homes, beautiful rag rugs cover the floors everywhere, including the hallways and staircases. Many of the tapestry rugs depict individuals wearing traditional Slovakian folk costumes and are rendered in wonderful detail and with tremendous overall energy. In Sweden, the tapestry technique, called *rolokan,* is often used to create images and colorful borders.

Tapestry, though a very old technique, can also be applied to the most current designs. Sara Hotchkiss creates exciting contemporary rugs that are alive with color and pattern. She draws on the Maine landscape and her flower gardens for inspiration, and her relationship with nature is evident in her rugs.

Tapestry also lends itself to geometric patterns. Lis Bech incorporates white cotton sheets, some of which she dyes to create contemporary rag rugs for the wall.

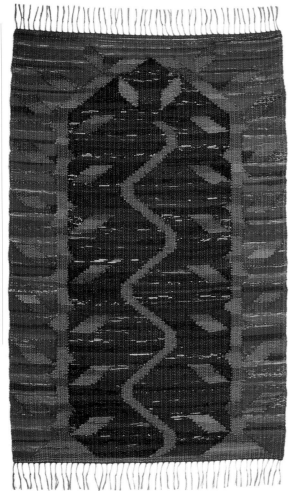

RIGHT:
Tree of Life,
**Sara Hotchkiss
(American), 48"
x 78" (122 x
198 cm), tapestry woven on a
multicolored
Parisian cotton
warp with cotton weft**
PHOTO: DENNIS
GRIGGS

FAR RIGHT:
Zig-Zag,
**Lis Bech
(Danish), 31½"
x 113½" (80 x
288 cm), tapestry-woven plain
weave on a
linen warp with
dyed cotton
weft**
PHOTO: OLE AKHØJ

INLAY

Inlay allows simple patterns and shapes to be created on the surface of the rug just under the warp. These rugs are generally one sided. Short strips of cloth are laid in on top of the regular weft and can create geometric style images and decorative color accents or borders. Often the tails, left about ½ inch (1.5 cm) long, are left protruding to contribute the effect of having pile within the design element.

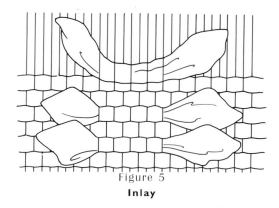

Figure 5

Inlay

Inlay done with strong pictorial sensitivity is seen in the work of Missy Stevens. (See her project in chapter 7.) Using the traditional inlay technique—without protruding tails—and a warp with a fine sett, she creates images with much more sensitivity than is possible with traditional tapestry weaving. Missy creates pictorial rugs for the wall as well as patterned designs for the floor. She works in recycled corduroy, which provides a palette of rich colors, and finishes her rugs with a Shaker-style four-strand braided border made of the same corduroy as her weft.

TUFTING & TATTER WEAVING

Within the realm of plain weave, the surface of a rug can be made more exciting by breaking out of the smooth, flat surface. Many early coverlets from Sweden, Canada, and Louisiana used simple techniques to vary the surface. Tripled or heavier weft strips create raised ribs or stripes, and tufting and inlay create decorative patterns.

In *Swedish tatter weave*, a continuous weft strip is laid in on top of the regular weft and held in place

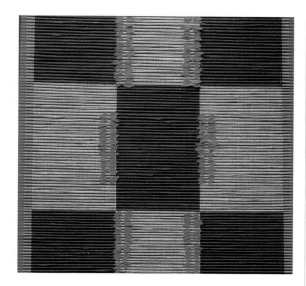

LEFT:
Detail of *Autumn Fields*, Gulvi Heed (Swedish), full size is 24¾" x 94½" (63 x 240 cm), cotton yarn warp, cotton yarn and rye straw weft, ribbed with cotton ribbon
PHOTO: HANS KONGBÄCK

BELOW:
Detail of *The All Stars*, Missy Stevens (American), full size is 36" x 60" (91.5 x 152.5 cm), mercerized cotton warp with cotton corduroy weft and inlay
PHOTO: WILLIAM B. SEITZ.

by a number of warp ends. The strip is then carried to the next shed and inlaid for a short segment. The resulting pattern can be based on either a contrasting color or the low relief created from the laid-in weft as it is carried from one shed to the

next. It is a form of inlay tapestry that allows designs to be created with a continuous strip of rag. This technique is visible only on one side, and the effect achieved is often very delicate, similar to white-on-white quilts.

Another design motif is the *boutonné* or button tufting seen in the coverlets in Canada. Small buttonlike projections are created by pulling a small loop of relaxed weft up from between the warp threads. The pulling can be repeated at intervals across the weft to create overall designs.

A highly textured tufted surface can be created by laying in or wrapping individual short strips of weft around one or two warp threads and allowing the ends to protrude. The short strips of weft are laid in by hand generally on a plain-weave rag ground, and additional pieces can be inserted later for accents when necessary. This technique is similar

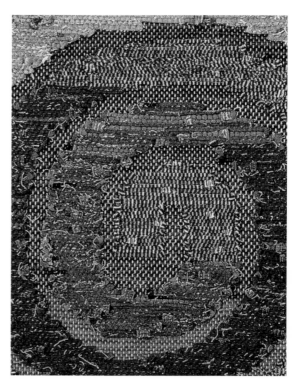

to Finnish rya rugs but uses fabric strips rather than wool yarn. When heavily tufted areas are combined with sections of traditional plain weave, a dramatic juxtaposition occurs.

Double corduroy and twice-woven rugs also have rich shag surfaces. See Wendy Bateman's project in chapter 7 for an example of the twice-woven technique.

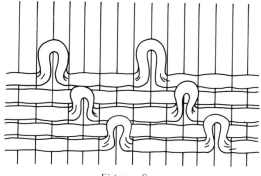

Figure 6
Boutonné

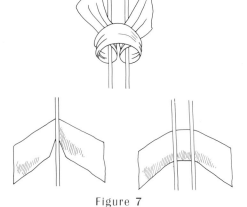

Figure 7
Tufting techniques

Weave Variations
▼

SQUARES

Just as the weft can be manipulated to create intriguing patterns, so can the warp provide many design options based on manipulating it through different weave structures. The square—an important building block of so many designs—is perfectly suited to the inherent weaving grid. There are numerous weave structures that create designs based on squares: log cabin, double bind, block weaves, and crackle weave are just a few.

Log Cabin

Log cabin is threaded by alternating one light thread and one dark thread. With each block, the order in which the colors alternate is reversed, creating interesting designs and color patterns. In general, log cabin creates a soft, gentle check. The combination of black and white is a popular choice, but there are many other possibilities for value

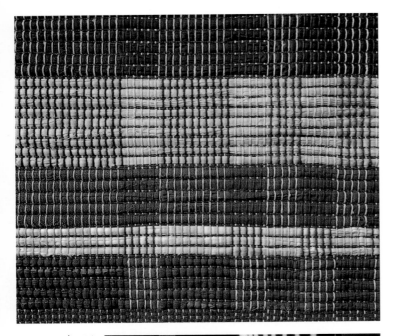

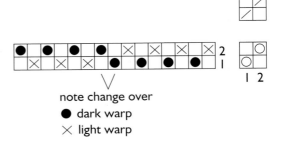

note change over

● dark warp

✕ light warp

Figure 8

Log cabin threading for two shafts

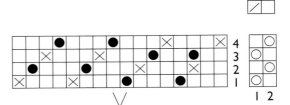

note change over

Figure 9

Log cabin threading for four shafts

When warping, the last thread color in each block is repeated once at the start of the next block. The two same-colored threads cause the light–dark sequence to reverse shafts, which allows the blocks to appear in the warp. Alternately, a contrasting third color can be used as the change-over thread. This creates a subtle overplaid.

Weaving is accomplished by using one or two rag shuttles and one boat shuttle wound with carpet warp. One shot of fabric is alternated with a shot of warp for the desired length of the block. To change the block, two consecutive shots of carpet warp or rag weft are woven.

Double Binding

Double binding allows you to create a reversible, double-sided geometric design, such as multiple squares, rectangles, or checkerboards. Double

contrasts, such as magenta and teal or rust and brilliant blue. With the log cabin technique, you can vary the width of blocks, create incremental increases in block size, use the Fibonacci series to size your blocks, alternate weft colors on two shuttles, use a Hit-and-Miss weft, and add other variations. Log cabin is an old favorite and makes a very flexible basic design.

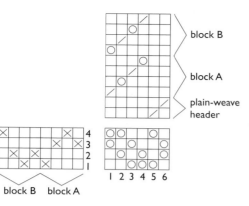

block B

block A

plain-weave
header

4
3
2
1

block B   block A

1 2 3 4 5 6

Figure 10
Double-bind threading

binding can create a much stronger block design than log cabin. Whereas log cabin produces the design on the surface by warp manipulation, double binding creates designs through loom-controlled weft manipulation. Known as *taqueté* in Swedish, double binding is a very popular technique, since it allows for so many possibilities.

Double binding is a double-faced block-weave structure that employs four shafts for plain weave and eight shafts for twill. Although it is threaded at 16 epi, only eight warp threads are visible at a time. The other eight are hiding one shaft of the weft and causing it to appear on the reverse face, thus creating a reversible rug that has the opposite colors on each side. Rag strips in two colors are alternated until a block reaches the desired length, including take-up. At the end of each block, the last weft color is repeated once—giving two light or two dark wefts in a row—before alternating colors are resumed. Throughout the changes in weft, the treadle sequence is never broken. The top weft should cover the underlying weft, but if you use weft strips in varied widths, the underlying color will peek through occasionally, creating a rich surface.

Double binding can also be used in combination with draw devices. A draw device is a supplemen-

tal warp-lifting mechanism that allows the weaver to lift certain threads in addition to the manipulations resulting from threading and treadling. Liv Brugge's *Jasmine* is a wonderful illustration of the energy and narration that is possible with double binding. Liv used double binding in combination with draw devices for her design.

In addition to log cabin and double binding, there are numerous other weave structures that create reversible geometric designs. They range in complexity and can require from four shafts to many more. Representative of the level of sophistication possible are the works of Claudia Mills. Claudia works with log cabin threading plus four-end block-weave structures. (A four-end block is a unit weave that uses four threads per basic unit. There are many different block weaves.) Claudia's choice in weave structures conveys the angularity of architecture that she cites as one of her inspirations.

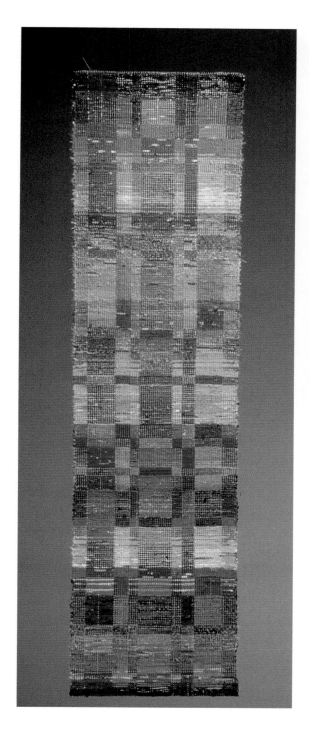

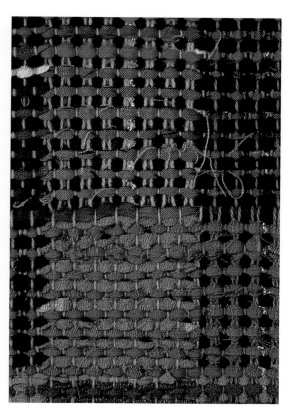

Her contemporary designs utilize new fabrics and create very distinctive floor coverings. (See her project in chapter 7.)

Jane Doyle of Roxbury, Connecticut, works with Summer and Winter, a variation of a four-end block weave. Summer and Winter is a very old weave structure that produces a reversed image on the opposite side of the rug. The sturdiness, reversibility, and design possibilities are what draw her to this weave pattern. Her project rug in chapter 7, shown there in two color variations, illustrates how two rugs can appear very different even when they're woven in the same warp and weave pattern. There you can see the difference between choosing color contrasts—teal and purple—and value contrasts—teal and taupe.

There are many variations possible with the basic idea of Summer and Winter. Gisela Von Weisz incorporates it with taqueté to create images. Karen Olesen Jakse uses crackle weave, a variation of Summer and Winter, to create rich surfaces that are built upon the basic square. Her recent work incorporates crackle with narrow strips of plain weave.

Multiple Techniques

Using two or more different techniques in a single design can result in rugs that are quietly powerful. Chad Alice Hagen combines double binding with weft gradations to create a rug with a sense of spa-

RIGHT:
DB #16,
**Chad Alice
Hagen**
(American),
38" x 87" (96.5
x 221 cm), dou-
ble bind, cotton
warp and cot-
ton corduroy
weft
PHOTO: NELL YTSMA

BELOW RIGHT:
*Standing White
Square,*
Viveka Nygren
(Swedish), 55"
x 55" (140 x
140 cm), twill
with tapestry
insert, 8/5 linen
warp,
unbleached
cotton rags and
silk and linen
yarn weft
PHOTO: KENT
HÖGLUND

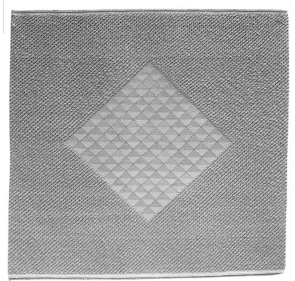

tial illusion and very strong graphics. Viveka Nygren contrasts the sturdy surface of rag weaving with an inset area of tapestry-woven plain weave, and the simplicity of her white palette emphasizes her materials and weaving structure. This surface contrast is also used by Lorraine Lamothe in *Bugs in a Rug I: Mictis Profana.* There the subtlety of the blue border and corner area woven of yarn underscores the richness of the surface of the weft-faced tapestry-woven areas.

In addition to their potential variations in weaving, rag rugs also provide a unique surface on which to add further decoration. Applying surface design techniques to rag rugs—a practice considered by

many to be contemporary— actually has a significant history. *American Rugs and Carpets* by Helen Von Rosenstiel shows a rag rug from the first half of the 19th century that has been stenciled with columns of pineapples and stripes. At a time when painted floorcloths were common and surface design techniques—especially stenciling—were well known, rag rugs were natural candidates for embellishment.

The current blurring of the boundaries between weaving and surface design suggests that there may be more nonwoven design techniques applied to rag rugs in the future. Master weaver Jane Evans uses several methods to create surface designs or images on her rag rugs. She works with painted warps, rag wefts, and a split-shed method of weaving. Using commercially printed fabrics and specific weaving techniques, she is able to retain the surface or pictorial design of the fabric within the rug.

Due to their size and weight, rag rugs are not very conducive to immersion dyeing or other techniques that require extensive rinsing or manipulation in water. Despite the obvious drawbacks, I began painting my rag rugs with fabric dyes several years ago. (See my project in chapter 7.) For rinsing some of the larger rugs, I use horse-watering tanks and a small pony pump to drain out the water. Rinsing can take five or six days, depending on the size of the rug and the values of the dyes

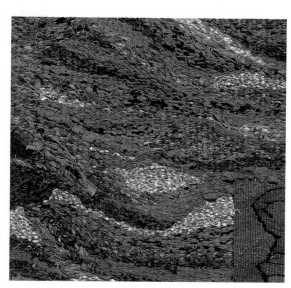

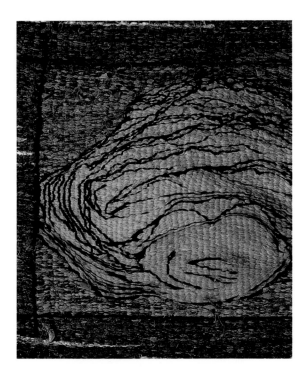

used—deeper values generally require longer rinsing times. Though the dyeing process often consumes more time than weaving the rug, I am excited by the strong physical quality of the rag surface for receiving imagery, color, and pattern.

Others share my enthusiasm for combining surface design with rag rug weaving. Australian textile artist Valeska Siddall works on the woven rag rug surface after it is off the loom, incorporating indigo dyeing, screen printing, masking, and hand application of textile inks to create layered surfaces that echo the palette and layered surfaces of the Australian earth. Through her surface design, she is able to convey a sense of environmental forces or turbulence. She also uses areas of tapestry inlay to create the impression of windows and contrasting surfaces.

In Finland, Raili Ruppa weaves dense weft-faced rugs, using imported denim that she has custom dyed. Her rugs are woven in plain weave, and she uses a modified screen printing technique to create very striking asymmetrical images on the surface. Music and the Finnish countryside inspire her colors and designs.

Computer-Assisted Designs

As in many other fields, the growth of computer technology is already having a major impact on new designs for rag rugs. Wendy Regier begins by drawing designs on graph paper; then she manipulates the shapes and designs on her computer. The resulting rugs have a very contemporary feeling to them.

Sara Lindsay uses the symbolic nature and texture of cloth, particularly black-and-white gingham, which she scans into her computer and manipulates. Her designs incorporate ideas—such as memory and returning home—and issues relating to migrants. She works in the tapestry tradition and approaches her rag weaving from a theoretical and formal, fine-art perspective.

This chapter has touched upon just a handful of the design variations available to you. Sample the projects in chapter 7, study the works of other rag weavers, and consult several of the many good weaving texts for other design ideas. By combining different techniques or working with old standby methods in fresh, new ways, you'll find that there are tremendous possibilities for your rag rugs. Experiment with these possibilities and allow them to take you in exciting, new directions.

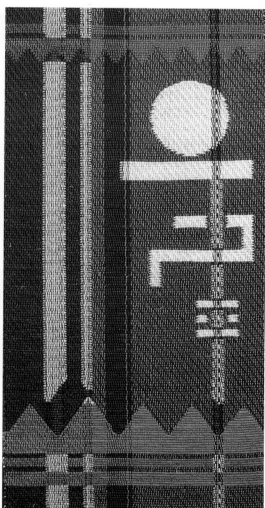

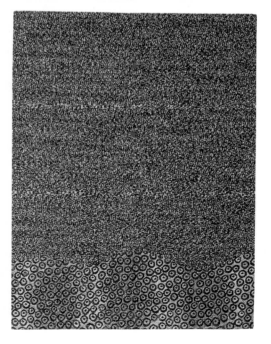

VI

FINISHING THE RUG

After many hours, weeks, or possibly months of weaving, the next step is to cut the rug from the loom. This is an exciting time, with a level of anticipation similar to that of opening a present. Now you get to see what your efforts have produced, its overall effect, and how your rug looks on the floor.

▼

After your initial feelings of pride and creative ownership have abated, assess the rug from an objective standpoint. Evaluate the weaving, addressing elements such as straight selvages, actual versus expected length, color and composition, quality of craftsmanship, and overall feeling. Especially when you are beginning, it's a good idea to make notes in your sketchbook, recording elements that were successful, those that didn't work as hoped, and ideas for future rugs. Once the rug is finished and blocked, take a photograph for further reference. This, along with the actual fabric swatches stapled in your notebook, will become invaluable for future reference.

RIGHT:
Autumn Rising I,
Sara Hotchkiss
(American), 60"
x 66" (152.5 x
167.5 cm),
tapestry woven
on a multicol-
ored Parisian
cotton warp
with cotton
weft
PHOTO: DENNIS
GRIGGS

As you look it over carefully, you may notice short protrusions of fabric on the surface of your rug. These are referred to as ears, tails, nubs, or stubs, and they result from how the weft strips were cut, joined, or laid in during the weaving process.

Depending on the look you want to achieve, they may be left as a natural by-product of the weaving process or trimmed off. When trimming, use a pair of sharp scissors and take extreme care not to snip any warp threads.

Finishing Techniques

The simplest and easiest way to end a rug is to make a knotted fringe. After laying the rug flat on a work surface, take groups of eight threads and knot them in over-hand knots, pushing the knots right up next to the rug and pulling snugly. Begin in the center and work outward to the edges to help prevent uneven draw-in of the fringe.

To cut your fringe, lay the rug flat on a table and square the rug along one side of the table, with the desired fringe line right at the edge of the table. Comb the fringe so that it looks even. Now line up the scissors along the edge of the edge of the table and cut, running the scissors along the table edge

Finishing techniques (clockwise, starting at top left): rolled hem, finger-woven edge, twisted or plied fringe, Damascus edge, four-strand braid, and braided fringe

as a guide. This will give you an even fringe. At this point, you can use a liquid fray retardant to keep the fringe looking like new through multiple washings and years of wear.

A more elaborate fringe can be made by alternating overhand knots. After making the initial line of knots along the edge of the rug, split each group of threads in half and tie the adjacent halves together to make a second row of knots. Then divide these

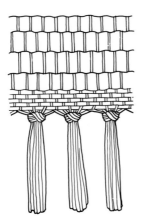

Thread them through the last bit of the header and incorporate them evenly across the fringe. To determine how many threads you should add, a general rule of thumb is to be able to gather the fringe threads in groups of six or eight. With a wide sett, a group of eight would span a distance that might cause pull-in or leave long warp threads exposed to wear. Try different fringe densities to see what works best.

A favorite finishing technique, having better wearability than the simple fringe, is the twisted or plied fringe. Working in two groups of four, take one group in each hand and tightly twist it in the same direction that the thread is twisted. Then place the two groups together and tightly twist in the opposite direction. Finish with a knot at the bottom.

Various braids may serve as decorative elements as well as methods for preserving the fringe. Three-strand braids are simple to do, but more complex

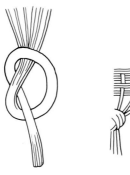

Figure 1
Simple knotted fringe

groups in half and repeat the process for a third row. (See figure 2.)

If you have used a wide sett for your warp, you will need to supplement your fringe with additional threads. The added warp threads should be a little more than double the length of the existing fringe.

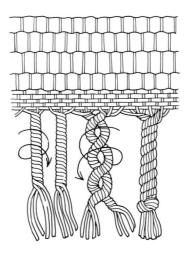

Figure 3
Twisted or plied fringe

braids tend to lie flatter. Rather than having conventional fringe, the Shakers framed their rugs with multiple-strand braids made of fabric strips.

To weave a four-strand braid, the strand on the left is woven over, under, and over to become the strand on the right. Repeat, always starting from the left. Figure 5 illustrates how to make a four-

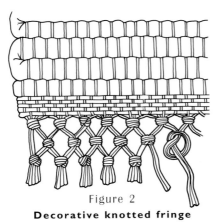

Figure 2
Decorative knotted fringe

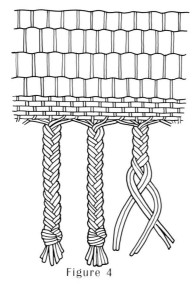

Figure 4

Three-strand braid

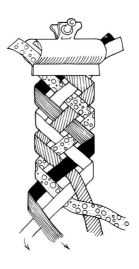

Figure 5

Four-strand braid

strand braid with fabric strips, but the over-under-over sequence is the same for a four-strand braided fringe. However, due to the thinness of the warp thread, the strands should be doubled to produce a good braid.

Another option is a finger-woven edge. This is an excellent way of finishing a rug, but you may need some practice before you can do it perfectly. Lay the rug flat on a table and align the edge of the rug with the edge of the table for your guide. Place a heavy weight on the rug or secure it in some manner so that it won't move as you weave the edging.

Begin by creating a corner, using a piece of the warp thread approximately 12 inches (30.5 cm) long as your weft. Finger-weave the supplemental weft thread as shown in step 1 of figure 6 and push the finger-woven weft against the rug to form a wedge-shaped corner.

Now finger-weave the warp as shown in step 2. Once each warp-turned-weft thread is woven into the desired six warp ends, pick up a new end. Follow the fell of the rug, but leave enough room widthwise so that the ends may be threaded back through the woven edge as shown in step 3. The remaining ends on the right-hand side may be plaited into a decorative braid that hangs to the side of

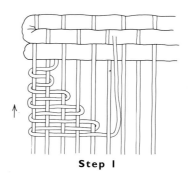

Step 1

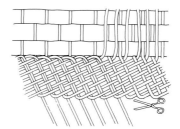

Step 2

Step 3

Figure 6

Finger-woven edge

the rug. The warp ends are now threaded back through, using a tapestry needle or crochet hook. You may also need pliers to coax the needle through the woven edge. When all the warp ends have been woven back, trim the ends as close as possible to the woven edge.

The Damascus edge is a simple yet sophisticated finishing technique. Working from right to left with a passive warp thread in your left hand and an active thread in your right, knot over and up. Then turn back and work your way across again. After the second pass, the thread ends will face down, allowing them to be knotted, plied, braided, or simply worked back into the body of the rug with a needle.

Another nonprotruding and simple edging technique is the rolled hem. For a sewn rolled hem, carefully roll the rug into a log as it is taken off the loom. To hold the warp in place until it is sewn, run a bead of liquid fray retardant along the edge of the header. Then set your sewing machine to have a fairly wide zigzag stitch and a medium number of stitches per inch and sew just at the edge of the woven header. I center my sewing machine along the edge of a table; the table serves as a support for the entire rug roll, and I just slide it along the table as I am sewing. I usually stand while doing this. Finish one edge; then rewind the rug to get to the other end. Repeat with another line of sewing on each end.

A triple thickness of the header will create a hem that is comparable in thickness with the woven body of the rug. Divide the header into thirds, turn it under, and pin it in place. It can be stitched by hand, using some of the warp thread, or sewn by machine with sewing thread. See figure 8.

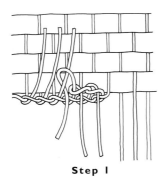

Step 1

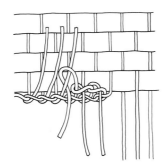

Step 2

Figure 7
Damascus edge

Blocking

The final step, after completing the fringe or edging, is to block your rug. Though we strive to weave very straight, tight, square rugs, they don't always come off the loom that way. Sometimes allowing a rug to relax and lie flat on the floor for a couple days will be enough to straighten it. Other rugs may require blocking.

To block a rug, you will need a sturdy blocking surface. I've found the best material to be a sheet of homasote (the material generally used to make bulletin boards) because it will accept T-pins inserted by hand. If you use a sheet of plywood, then you will need a hammer and rustproof nails. Your blocking surface should be as large as possible, prefer-

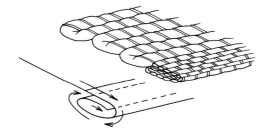

Figure 8
Rolled hem

ably 4 by 8 feet (1.2 by 2.4 m). You will also need a sheet of plastic larger than the rug (the same size as your blocking surface is ideal), a large metal L- or T-square, a metal ruler at least 36 inches (91.5 cm) long, large T-pins or a hammer and nails, and a spray bottle filled with water.

The rug must be thoroughly dampened before it can be pulled into shape. You can use the spray bot-

tle, wetting the rug as you work, or you can place the rug in a washing machine to dampen it all at once. If you choose the second method, use warm water and the gentle cycle.

Place the sheet of plastic on top of your blocking surface to protect it from moisture.

To begin blocking, line up one selvage with the long

If the rug wasn't dampened in a washing machine, spray it as needed to make it wet. Areas that bubble up as you are blocking will settle down once they are sprayed with water. For this to work, you must get all the fibers wet, not just lightly misted.

Once the rug is blocked, the homasote or plywood can be stood on end to allow the excess water to drain off the rug. This will provide better ventilation and shorten the drying time. Depending on the time of year, placing your rug outdoors in the sun can speed the drying tremendously. The layer of plastic under the rug also helps to accelerate the drying time.

After the rug has dried, remove the pins. Now your rug is ready for the floor! If it is to go on a smooth or hard surface such as wood, stone, or brick, consider placing a pad underneath it. A rug pad provides more comfort, prevents the rug from skidding across the floor, and cushions the rug from any unevenness below. There are many different types of rug pads available; the plastic-coated open-grid style is fairly unobtrusive and works very well.

If you don't plan to use your rug right away or want to ship it somewhere else, always make sure that it is rolled rather than folded when you transport or store it. Roll the rug in the same direction as it was rolled on the beam of the loom.

edge of the blocking surface. Starting at one end of the rug, set the L- or T-square so that the short arm rests along the long edge of the blocking surface and the longer arm extends across the end of the rug. Now place the ruler so that it extends the line of the L-square along the end of the rug. Running along the line made by the L-square and ruler, insert T-pins to secure the end of the rug to the blocking surface.

Move the L-square and ruler about 3 inches (7.5 cm) and pin across again, starting in the center of the rug and following a weft outward to the selvages. Insert the T-pins between weft shots, following the line of the L-square and ruler. Continue pinning every 3 inches (7.5 cm) down the body of the rug.

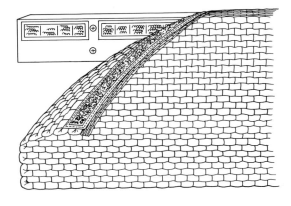

Figure 9

Hanging the rug with hook and loop tape

82

Wall Presentation

These days many rag rugs find their way to the wall rather than the floor. With a wall installation, the appearance and craftsmanship of the hanging mechanism becomes as important as the rug itself. The easiest and least obtrusive way to hang even a large rug is to use hook and loop tape. Use tape that is 1 or 2 inches (2.5 or 5 cm) wide, depending on the size of the rug. For rugs 6 by 8 feet (1.8 by 2.4 m) or larger, use 2-inch (5-cm) tape or two strips of 1-inch (2.5-cm) tape. When purchasing hook and loop tape for this purpose, always choose a quality brand, such as Velcro, that has good strength.

Due to the stiffness of the hook and loop tape, it is easier to sew it to strips of blanket tape or other nonstretch fabric tape before attaching it to the rug. Sew the loop portion of the hook and loop tape to the blanket tape. Position the blanket tape about ½ inch (1.5 cm) down from the top of the rug and ½ inch (1.5 cm) in from each side; then sew around the edge of the blanket tape (fig. 9).

The hook portion of the tape is attached to a piece of wood ¼ inch (5 mm) thick by 1½ or 2 inches (4 or 5 cm) wide and about 1 inch (2.5 cm) shorter than the width of the rug. Sand the wood lightly and paint it with two coats of paint to seal the wood so that it won't warp over time. For best results, use paint that matches your wall color. Predrill and countersink screw holes in the wooden hanging strip to prevent the wood from splitting during the installation process. Cut the hook portion of the tape to fit the wood and staple it along the top edge. Then, using a hammer, tap each staple to fit snugly.

To hang your rug, determine where you want the top of the rug to be and install the wooden board ½ inch (1.5 cm) down from this height. Lightly press the rug onto its hanger. Then step back, look at it from a distance, and make any necessary adjustments by pulling back one edge and easing it into the desired position.

Other, less permanent hanging methods are also available. Jutta Graf drills holes in a thin piece of

Color Library, **Heather Allen, 69" x 90" (175 x 228.5 cm), canvas appliqué, painted dyes, screened and printed textile inks, cotton warp and weft**
PHOTO: JOHN LUCAS

lath and attaches her rug to the wooden strip with large stitches made of warp thread or heavy string. This allows the rug to be displayed on the wall and easily removed for use on the floor. Another possibility is to weave a header about 3 or 4 inches (7.5 or 10 cm) on one end, then sew it into a tube. Leave the ends open to accommodate a wooden dowel or metal rod. Any wooden hanging mechanisms should always be painted or varnished to prevent warping and to give a more professional appearance.

One way to hang a rug without sewing anything to it is to use carpet strips. These are strips of heavy composition board with tacks protruding every inch (2.5 cm). Carpet strips are available from carpet stores, or you can make your own by driving fine nails through thin pieces of lath. Fasten the carpet strip to the wall and carefully hang your rug on the protruding tacks or nails. (This method is handy for temporarily hanging a rug you want to photograph.)

These are just a few examples of how you might display your rug on a wall. Whenever you visit art galleries or shops, take note of how rugs and other textiles are presented.

VII

RAG RUG
PROJECTS

▼

In Bloom

Design by Wynne Mattila

Cotton fabrics in twelve color values and an alternating three-shuttle technique are used in this plain-weave rug. Stripes progress from dark to light to dark again in a subtle gradation of tones. Each stripe is created by blending three fabrics that work together to create a sense of depth. In the center of the rug, where the palest stripes meet, is an area filled with light and airiness. The finished size is 29 by 68½ inches (.7 by 1.7 m) with 5½ inches (14 cm) of braided fringe at each end.

Equipment

Four-shaft two-treadle loom, #10 or #5 reed at least 32 inches (81.5 cm) wide, 12 stick shuttles, temple, warp separator sticks

Warp

515 yards (471 m) of natural-colored 15-ply cotton seine twine

Weft

New, all-cotton calico fabrics that have been washed, dried, and cut into 1-inch (2.5-cm) strips. You will need a total of at least 3¼ pounds (1.5 kg) of fabric in a range of 12 values of similar or analogous or harmonious colors. Quantities for each color are: 2 ounces (57 g) each of fabric 1—the darkest value—and fabric 12—the lightest value; 5 ounces (142 g) each of fabrics 2, 3, 4, 5, 6, 7, and 8; 6 ounces (170 g) of fabric 9; 4 ounces (114 g) of fabric 10; and 3 ounces (85 g) of fabric 11.

Take-Up

10 percent in length

Draw-In

9 percent in width

Warping

Wind 164 ends, using 5 epi and a width of 31½ inches (80 cm), with four ends for doubled floating selvages and four for doubled two-pattern threading at each edge. Warp length is 3⅓ yards (3 m), which includes take-up, shrinkage, and 36 inches (91.5 cm) of loom waste. Part of the loom waste is used for the fringe at each end.

Threading & Tie-Up

See the draft.

Sleying

Sley at 5 epi, with one end every other dent in the #10 reed or one end every dent in a #5 reed. Use doubled ends for the first two and last two pairs of working (pattern) warp threads; these are threaded singly through the heddles but doubled through the reed. Use floating doubled selvages—do not thread them through the heddles, but do thread them through the same dent in the reed. Do not skip a dent between the pattern ends and the floating selvages.

Weft Preparation

Wash the yardage in hot water and dry it on a hot setting in a dryer. Cut the fabric into 1-inch (2.5-cm) strips.

Weaving

Weave enough filler to spread the warp evenly. Then weave in the warp separator sticks to create

a straight fell line, eliminating any potential curve or "smile." Weave in sufficient additional filler to allow you to use the temple and weave a few picks of scrap yarn to help secure the weft when the rug is removed for finishing. A total of 9 inches (23 cm) of reserved warp is needed at each end for braiding the fringe.

Using a temple set at the width of the reed reduces wear on the outer warp threads and helps maintain the desired width. As you weave, the temple

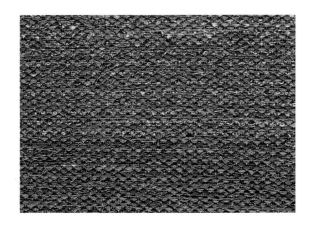

the right. When beating, position the weft in the shed, beat hard, open the shed, and beat quickly and firmly two more times. Lay shuttle 1 (fabric 1) on the woven web area. Weave a shot of fabric 2 from the left and place shuttle 2 below shuttle 1. Weave a shot of fabric 3 from the right and place shuttle 3 below shuttle 2. Always place the shuttle you have used last below the others or in the last position.

Continue this sequence, using fabrics 1, 2, and 3 for 3½ inches (9 cm); then replace fabric 1 with fabric 4 and weave 3½ inches (9 cm) with fabrics 2, 3, and 4. Drop fabric 2 and add fabric 5, weaving for 3½ inches (9 cm) with fabrics 3, 4, and 5. Continue weaving sections of 3½ inches (9 cm), dropping one fabric and adding another for sequences of fabrics 4–5–6, 5–6–7, 6–7–8, 7–8–9, 8–9–10, and 9–10–11.

Weave the center 3½ inches (9 cm) using fabrics 9, 11, and 12; then reverse the sequence to weave the rest of the rug (11–10–9, 10–9–8, 9–8–7, 8–7–6, 7–6–5, 6–5–4, 5–4–3, 4–3–2, and 3–2–1).

Finishing

Cut the rug from the loom, leaving 9-inch (23-cm) warp tails for the fringe. Allow the rug to relax on a flat surface for 24 hours before finishing the ends. Remove the few picks of scrap yarn and tie square knots across the width of the rug, using two warp ends to make each knot. Using groups of six warp ends, two ends per strand, make three-strand braids, each 3½ inches (9 cm) long, across both ends of the rug. Tie each braid in an overhand knot at the end and trim the ends evenly, allowing 1½ inch (4 cm) for fringe.

should be moved about every inch (2.5 cm), and the warp tension should be very tight. The treadling is consistent for the entire rug: treadle 1, treadle 2. To change fabrics, taper the ends and overlap the weft strips for about 2 inches (5 cm) while in the same raised shed. *In Bloom* is woven at 7 picks per inch (2.5 cm).

To create a clean selvage, Wynne uses the three-shuttle technique with floating selvages. When weaving with floating selvages, the shuttle goes over the floating selvage on the way into the shed and under the floating selvage on the way out of the shed. A small note (in − over, out − under) tacked to the castle can help to keep this straight.

Begin the body of the rug by weaving a header of four doubled picks of the 15-ply warp thread. Wind the twelve fabrics on the twelve stick shuttles and start weaving with a shot of fabric 1 from

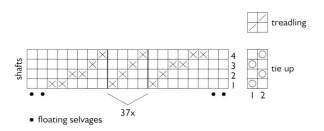

KATHY'S GARDEN

Design by Debra Sharpee

This rug is a variation of the "Diamond Rug," woven in plain weave in *Rag Rug Handbook* by Janet Meany and Paula Pfaff. In the original design, diamond shapes are created by using fabrics of the same width that are stitched together, cut into strips, and woven into a shifting pattern. The use of a repeat slightly less than twice the width of the rug creates diagonals throughout the textile. This variation uses different widths of fabric to create accents and variation within the rug. The finished size is 29 by 43½ inches (73.5 by 110.5 cm).

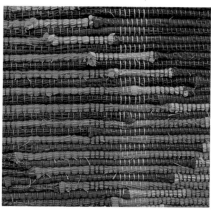

Equipment & Supplies

Two-shaft two-treadle loom with a minimum weaving width of 30 inches (76 cm), #12 reed, ski shuttles, sewing machine, sewing thread, fabric glue

Warp

This rug uses 8/4 cotton carpet warp, and you will need 420 yards (385 m) of royal blue, 80 yards (74 m) of burgundy, 120 yards (110 m) each of bright blue and aqua green, and 160 yards (147 m) of light teal green.

Weft

Washed corduroy in the following colors: 7 square feet (6512 sq cm) of hot pink, 10 square feet (.9 sq m) of lime green, 14 square feet (1.3 sq m) of aqua, 4½ square feet (4190 sq cm) of dark gold, and 8½ square feet (7910 sq cm) of forest green

Take-Up

10 percent in length

Draw-In

3 percent in width

Warping

Wind a symmetrically striped 2½-yard-long (2.3-m) warp in the following colors: 48 ends of royal blue, 6 ends of light teal green, 12 ends of aqua green, 6

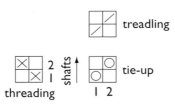

threading
2 1 shafts
treadling
tie-up
1 2

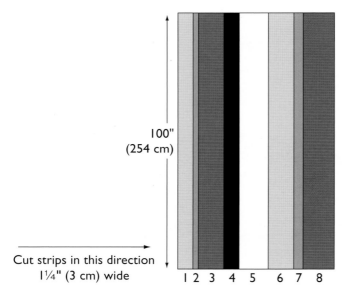

100"
(254 cm)

Cut strips in this direction
1¼" (3 cm) wide

1 2 3 4 5 6 7 8

Strip no.	Width after piecing inches (cm)	Piece color
1	5¾ (14.5)	hot pink
2	2 (5)	lime green
3	9½ (24)	aqua
4	5¾ (14.5)	dark gold
5	11 (28)	lime green
6	9 ½ (24)	aqua
7	3 ½ (9)	hot pink
8	11¾ (30)	forest green
	58¾ (149)	total width of piece

Figure 1

Weft Preparation

ends of light teal green, 8 ends of burgundy, 32 ends of bright blue, 8 ends of burgundy, 6 ends of light teal green, 12 ends of aqua green, 6 ends of light teal green, 72 ends of royal blue, 6 ends of light teal green, 12 ends of aqua green, 6 ends of light teal green, 8 ends of burgundy, 32 ends of bright blue, 8 ends of burgundy, 6 ends of light teal green, 12 ends of aqua green, 6 ends of light teal green, and 48 ends of royal blue, for a total of 360 ends.

Threading & Tie-Up

Thread for plain weave; see the draft.

Sleying

Center the warp with 12 epi; sley one end per dent.

Weft Preparation

Using a ½-inch (1.5-cm) seam allowance, stitch the fabric pieces together as shown in figure 1. Cut and stitch the pieces as necessary to create long rectangular shapes. To create the weft strips, cut the pieced fabric block horizontally into 1¼-inch (3-cm) strips. Wind the strips onto shuttles, taking care to keep the order of the colors. When winding the shuttles, always start with the same color—such as the hot pink—and finish with the color from the opposite side of the strip—such as forest green.

Weaving

Weave a 3-inch (7.5-cm) header of plain weave, using tripled 8/4 warp. Run a line of fabric glue along the start of the hem and allow it to dry. Weave the complete rug in plain weave with the rag weft, paying special attention to the color order. End by weaving a 3-inch (7.5-cm) header with the tripled 8/4 warp. Again run a line of fabric glue along the end of the hem.

Finishing

Remove the rug from the loom and machine-stitch the raw ends. Turn under each hem twice and stitch carefully along the fold line.

TWICE-WOVEN CHAIR PAD

Design by Wendy Bateman

This highly textured chair pad provides an opportunity to try the twice-woven rug technique on a project that won't take you too long to complete. It features a Hit-and-Miss color design, using a continuous rotation of wool strips done in chenille caterpillar strip weaving. These strips are then woven into a plain-weave base for the finished 13-by-13-inch (33-by-33-cm) chair pad or mat.

Making the Chenille Caterpillars

Equipment

Any small table loom that can weave a four-shed plain weave, #8 reed

Warp

Any recycled fine cotton or linen in 8/2 to 16/2 size

Weft

Recycled closely woven wool coats and blankets

Take-Up

Approximately 10%—weave 20 yards (18.3 m) of strips to obtain 18 yards (16.5 m) for weaving the chair pad

Draw-In

Negligible, due to the nature of the weave

Warping

Wind 96 ends for a warp 2½ yards (2.3 m) long.

Sleying

Sley at 8 epi, but place four threads each in two dents and leave six empty. The total width in the reed is 12 inches (30.5 cm). The length to weave the chenille strips is: 12 strips x 1⅔ yards (1.5 m) = 20 yards (18.3 m) of caterpillars for one chair pad.

Threading & Tie-Up

See the draft.

Weft Preparation

The wool coats and blankets must be washed and felted in the dryer before cutting. Cut them into strips ⅜ to ½ inch (1 to 1.5 cm) wide.

Weaving

Lay the strips in the warp, leaving a 1-inch (2.5-cm) overhang at each selvage edge. Every 5 inches (12.5 cm), stop and carefully cut the strips apart between the warp spaces. (See the detail photo at left.)

Finishing

Tie off both ends of the warp threads on each separate strip to prevent the caterpillars from unraveling.

Weaving the Chair Pad

Equipment

Four-shaft six-treadle loom that is at least 15 inches (38 cm) wide, #8 reed, heavy rug fork

Warp

4/8 high-twist cotton, doubled in the heddles and reed

Weft

Chenille caterpillars from the first weaving—they may need a good shake-out before weaving

Take-Up

10 percent in length

Draw-In

Less than 5 percent in width

Warping

Each pad needs only ½ yard (45.5 cm) of warp plus 1½ inches (4 cm) for the hems woven on each end.

Threading and Tie-up

See the draft.

Sleying

Two threads every second dent; the width in the reed is 13½ inches (34 cm) and becomes 13 inches (33 cm) once off the loom.

Weaving

Using doubled warp threads, weave a 1½-inch (4-cm) header for the hem. Proceed to place the chenille strips into the shed. Pull the beater part way; then use a heavy rug fork to make the chenille weft stand up so that it won't get trapped in the shed when beaten. Beat firmly into place. Change sheds and beat firmly again. Do not overlap the caterpillars due to their thickness; wrap them around the selvage and tuck the ends back into the web. Keep the selvages even and make the turns so that your warp doesn't draw in at the sides. Continue weaving to the desired length. Tuck the last strip back into the last warp and weave a 1½-inch (4-cm) header for the other hem.

Finishing

Machine-stitch the edges of the hems with a narrow straight stitch. Fold in ½ inch (1.5 cm) and stitch again. Fold again and hand-stitch the final hem against the chair pad.

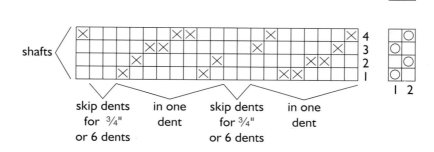

shafts

skip dents for ¾" or 6 dents | in one dent | skip dents for ¾" or 6 dents | in one dent

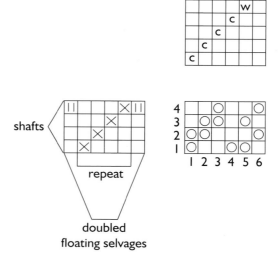

shafts

repeat

doubled
floating selvages

93

STRIPES WITH BLOCK BORDER

Design by Sara Hotchkiss

This simple yet effective design gains its drama from an imaginative choice of colors. Measuring 24½ by 50 inches (62 by 127 cm) plus 6 inches (15 cm) of fringe, it is a tapestry-woven rag rug with a block border and central area of stripes. The warp is threaded in log cabin blocks, using contrasting light and dark warp colors.

Equipment

Two-shaft two-treadle loom, #10 reed at least 30 inches (76 cm) wide, one boat shuttle for the headers, and two rag shuttles—one for each stripe color

Warp

Forest green, dark olive, beige, and light sand cotton carpet warp

Weft

Cotton fabric in two shades of fuchsia and two shades of pine green for the border blocks, one shade of pale chartreuse for the corner blocks, two shades of pine green for the center stripes, and two shades of bark for the center stripes

Take-Up

8 percent in length

Draw-In

3 percent in width

Warping

Wind 261 warp threads in total to give a warp 24½ inches (62 cm) wide at 10 epi, plus two heddles with four warp threads at each selvage. The warp is wound in the sequence of the four warp colors for block 1: forest green, beige, dark olive, and light sand. For block 2, the order is reversed, as shown in the draft. Repeat the two-block design across the warp.

Threading & Tie-Up

See the draft.

Sleying

Sley at 10 e.p.i. with two heddles having four warp threads at each selvage.

Weft Preparation

Machine wash and dry the fabric before cutting it into strips that average a pencil thickness. Cut widths of 1½ inches (4 cm) if the fabric is lightweight and ½ inch (1.5 cm) for fabric that is as heavy as flannel. The lengths for the center stripes are sewn end to end and wound on a shuttle in preparation for weaving.

Weaving

Weave 10 rows of header, using one of the warp colors. To weave the body of the rug, begin laying in strips of fuchsia, pine green, and fuchsia in 3-inch (7.5-cm) increments, making a total of eight blocks. Change colors at the beginning and end of each block by cutting a 1½-inch (4-cm) tail, wrapping it around the outside warp, and tucking it back into the weaving. Tuck in the tails of each block in the same shed. Using the dovetailing tapestry technique as described in chapter 5, weave the blocks for 3 inches (7.5 cm), creating a border of 3-inch (7.5-cm) blocks that alternate in color.

After the first row of blocks has been completed, change fabrics to create a green border block, then an accent chartreuse block. The central area is woven in 1-inch (2.5-cm) stripes—approximately five picks each—with three stripes per border block. At the left edge of the rug, lay in a chartreuse block and the fuchsia border block. Weave for 3 inches (7.5 cm), creating a border block and three stripes in the central area.

Now change the border block colors and expand the central stripes to fill in the area that contained the accent blocks in the previous section. Continue weaving 3-inch (7.5-cm) blocks and central stripes until you have woven 45 inches (114.5 cm) or 15 blocks. Then introduce the chartreuse accent blocks and finish the rug to mirror the other end.

Finishing

Using an overhand knot, tie the ends in groups of 10. Separate the warp colors of each group into warm and cool tones, twisting each color section separately; then join the two sections and twist them in the reverse direction. Tie the ends using an overhand knot and trim the fringe to 1 or 2 inches (2.5 or 5 cm).

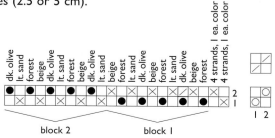

Repeat two-block design across warp

LADDER ESCAPE

Design by Heather Allen

The actual weaving for this rug is a very simple plain weave, and the main design elements are added off the loom. Relatively small in scale, it offers a good opportunity to try your hand at manipulating the surface quality of a rag rug by applying painted images to it. The design is created with fiber-reactive dyes and silkscreen textile inks, which reveal more or less of the underlying fabric colors, according to their translucence and density of application. The finished rug is 24 by 50 inches (61 by 127 cm).

Equipment

Four-shaft two-treadle loom; #10 reed 36 inches (91.5 cm) wide; boat shuttle; two rag or ski shuttles; standard sewing machine and industrial sewing machine; water-soluble fabric marker; dye activator; rubber gloves; respirator; reactive dyes in fuchsia, golden yellow, turquoise, and bright blue

Warp

8/4 all-cotton carpet warp in any medium to light values

Weft

Since the palette of the rug is primarily created through the dyes, any light- to medium-value weft will create a suitable foundation to accept the images. Fabrics with subtle patterns printed with dye or textile ink on white or light backgrounds can add interest to the surface of the rug. The dyes you will add are translucent, so the fabric will be transformed, not obscured.

Take-Up

20 percent in length

Draw-In

10 percent in width

Warping

Wind a 3-yard (2.8-meter) warp of 260 ends; this rug uses 10 red, 20 medium brown, 50 variegated brown and yellow, 100 yellow, 50 variegated brown and yellow, 20 medium brown, and 10 red.

Threading & Tie-Up

See the draft.

Sleying

One end per dent in a #10 reed

Weft Preparation

Cut the weft from a variety of all-cotton recycled fabrics into strips 1 to 1 1/2 inch (2.5 to 4 cm) wide, depending on the weight of the fabrics used. Machine-sew the strips together in the Hit-and-Miss style, taking care to spread the different fabrics throughout the body of the rug.

Weaving

Weave a 1 1/2-inch (4-cm) plain-weave header, using doubled red and brown warp thread. Weave the body of the rug in plain weave and repeat the header at the other end. Cut the rug off the loom, leaving the warp as though for a fringe. Using a zigzag stitch on the machine, sew the outer edges of the header. Trim off the excess warp.

Finishing

Fold the header into thirds and turn it under to create a rolled hem. Sew the hem by machine or by hand.

Preparation for Dye Painting

Draw a design on the rug with a water-soluble fabric marker. Using an industrial sewing machine and heavy-duty carpet thread, sew along the outlines of the drawing. This will serve as your guideline.

Applying the permanent image is a three-step process: activating the rug, painting in the design with the dyes, and curing the rug. You will be using room-temperature fiber-reactive dyes, so the temperature in the room throughout this process should always be above 70°F (21°C).

To activate the rug, mix a sufficient quantity of activator solution to submerse the rug, using 9 tablespoons (127.5 ml) of dye activator per gallon (3.8 l) of water. If you can't find dye activator, you can use the same proportion of soda ash or washing soda instead to make the solution. Soak the rug in the solution for 15 minutes; then remove it, without ringing it out, and hang it up to drip dry.

Dye Preparation & Painting

Following the manufacturer's instructions, prepare 2 quarts (1.9 l) of sodium alginate print paste. (PRO Chemical & Dye, Inc., sells a print paste mix that requires only the addition of water.) Mix the paste and let it stand for an hour.

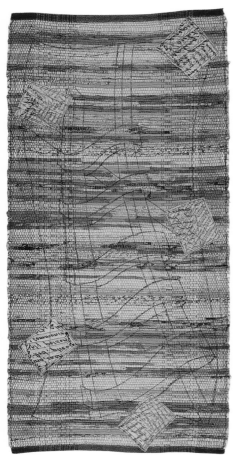

Using masking tape, label four 2-cup (473-ml) containers with the names of your colors: golden yellow, fuchsia, turquoise, and bright blue. The dyes are translucent and similar to watercolors, so I prepare the primary colors first, then mix the other colors I need from them. Due to the light value of turquoise, I usually mix two blues to get a shade I like.

Mix the stock colors using 2 teaspoons (10 ml) of dye per cup of paste. This is a good beginning range, and you can always lighten the colors later with plain print paste. Wearing rubber gloves and a respirator, carefully measure the dye. Powdered dye is hazardous material and, optimally, should be measured under an exhaust hood. It must always be treated with caution and respect. Make sure you have a wet sponge and a container of water nearby so that as soon as you are finished using a utensil it can be put directly into water and cleaned thoroughly afterwards. To mix the dye, put 1 tablespoon (15 ml) of water in each container and measure in the dye, stirring it gently to make sure it is well dissolved. Then add the print paste. To make sure the dye and paste have integrated well, allow the dye and paste to sit for one hour and stir before using.

The first time you use fabric dyes, it's a good idea to paint a sampler on a piece of scrap cloth that has been treated with dye activator. Label your sample so that you have a reference for future use.

Once you're ready, begin to paint the images, following your guidelines. Paint one side of the rug; then flip it and paint the other. I like to paint the same image but in reverse on the back side of the rug, but once you have an activated rug and the prepared dyes, you can be creative and paint whatever you want on each side. If you take a break between painting sessions, cover the rug with plastic.

Once both sides of the rug are painted and fairly dry, lay the rug flat on a piece of plastic that is wider and at least 2 feet (61 cm) longer than the rug. Dampen both sides with a spray bottle of water and roll the rug in the plastic so that there is a plastic buffer at all times and the rug never touches itself. Tape the ends closed and let it sit in a warm place for 24 hours.

After it has cured, unroll the rug and begin rinsing. I use a bathtub to immerse the rug in cold water until the water runs clear. This may require a day or two, with frequent water changes. Once the water rinses clear, change to hot water and rinse again until it is clear. In the last rinse, add a few drops of a gentle liquid dish detergent.

Lay the rug flat to dry and block if necessary. Additional surface design techniques, such as stenciling, silkscreening, and the direct application of textile inks or fabric paints can be done once the rug is completely dry. Refer to the manufacturer's instructions for the specific textile inks or fabric paints for the appropriate heat settings. The ladder in this design was further defined with silkscreened textile inks that were heat-set using an iron.

treadling

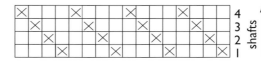

tie-up

98

NUMBER 261

Design by Claudia Mills

This is a reversible, four-end block-weave rug. The nature of this weave is that there is a hidden set of warp threads inside, and every other warp thread is visible on the surface. The color changes in the warp do not affect the weave structure at all; instead they add interest to the surface design. Claudia's colors change arbitrarily and don't correspond to her threading block changes. It may sound complicated, but it will all make sense once you begin weaving. The finished size is 34 by 26½ inches (86.5 by 67.5 cm).

Equipment

Four-shaft four-treadle loom, #8 reed 36 inches (91.5 cm) wide, one boat shuttle, two rag shuttles

Warp

8/4 rug warp in purple, green, yellow, and blue

Weft

Olive, navy, and light yellow fabric

Take-Up

10 percent in length

Draw-In

3 percent in width (start with 35 inches/89 cm and end with 34 inches/86.5 cm)

Warping

For an 8 epi warp, wind: 26 purple + 46 dark green + 40 blue + 6 light yellow+ 20 blue = 278 total ends. Warp length is 72 inches (1.8 m). The yarns on shafts 1 and 2 are the ones visible on the rug; the warp wound for shafts 3 and 4 are hidden within the rug, so you may use any leftover warp for that portion, if you desire. To do this, the surface warp numbers should be halved and the warp wound double—one colored warp and one "hidden" warp.

Threading & Tie-Up

See the draft.

Sleying

Sley at 8 epi. If you are using a different color for the inner warp, sley by alternating the internal or hidden color warp with the pattern warp.

Weft Preparation

Cut the fabric into strips 1½ to 2 inches (4 to 5 cm) wide, depending on the weight of the fabric. You want to produce between 3 and 4 picks per inch (2.5 cm).

Weaving

Weave a 2½-inch (6.5-cm) plain-weave header, using treadles 1 and 4 and blue warp thread doubled.

The threading for this rug allows for two blocks. There must be at least two shuttles in use at all times. One shuttle is for block A, and one is for block B.

Step 1: To weave the first 2 inches (5 cm), treadle 1 (raise shafts 2 and 4) and throw the yellow shuttle from the left side. Change shed with treadle 2 (raising shafts 2 and 3) and beat. Throw the olive green from the left side half of the way, cut the fabric strip at a tapered angle, overlap the tapered end of the navy strip of fabric for 3 inches (7.5 cm), and continue with the navy across. You have now completed one shot of block A and block B. Treadle 3 (raise shafts 1 and 4), beat, and from the right, throw the yellow shuttle. Treadle 4 (raise shafts 1 and 3) and beat. From the right, throw the navy shuttle half of the way, cut the navy strip at a tapered angle, and overlap it with the tapered tail of olive green. Continue across with the olive green. Continue weaving blocks A and B for 2 inches (5 cm).

Step 2: Weave the next 2 inches (5 cm) by treadling the same as above but using olive green in both shuttles. This is straight weaving, with no need to cut and overlap.

Step 3: Weave the next 12½ inches (31.5 cm) by following the same sequence and weft colors as used in step 1.

Step 4: Weave the next 2 inches (5 cm), using the same sequence and weft colors as used in step 2.

Step 5: Weave the next 6 inches (15 cm) in the same sequence and weft colors as used in step 1.

Step 6: Weave the next 2 inches (5 cm) by following the same sequence as step 2 but using two shuttles with navy wefts.

Weave a 2½-inch (6.5-cm) header using doubled blue warp thread.

Finishing

Using a sewing machine, secure the edge of the header with a zigzag stitch. Fold the header in thirds and turn it under; then machine-stitch with a straight stitch for a smooth finish.

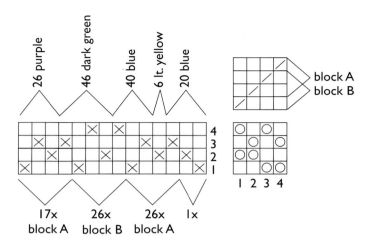

26 purple
46 dark green
40 blue
6 lt. yellow
20 blue

block A
block B

4
3
2
1

17x
block A

26x
block B

26x
block A

1x

1 2 3 4

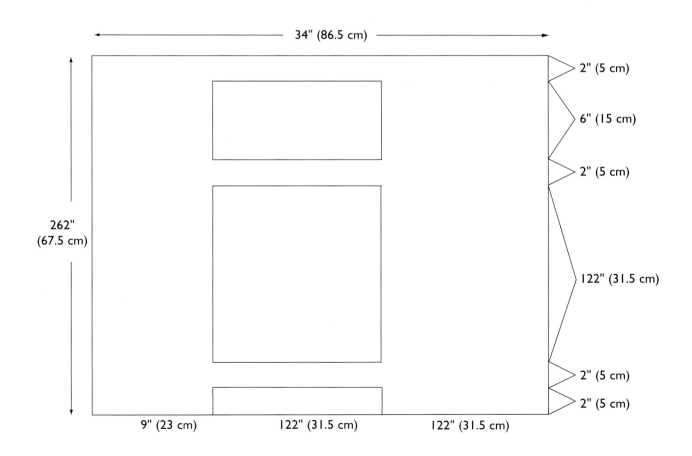

34" (86.5 cm)

262"
(67.5 cm)

2" (5 cm)

6" (15 cm)

2" (5 cm)

122" (31.5 cm)

2" (5 cm)

2" (5 cm)

9" (23 cm)   122" (31.5 cm)   122" (31.5 cm)

ORIENTAL GOLD

Design by Beth Hatton

As gentle in tone as the morning sun, this rug demonstrates how a thoughtful selection of colors can bring elegance to a simple checkerboard motif. It is woven in a four-end block weave also known as Summer and Winter, which produces a reversed image on the other side of the rug. Because of its narrow sett, this is a weft-faced rug. Its finished size is 33 by 60 inches (84 by 152.5 cm).

Equipment

Four-shaft six-treadle loom, #6 reed (or use a #12 reed and skip every other dent) at least 36 inches (91.5 cm) wide, three shuttles—two for plain weave and one for block weave

Warp

Natural linen 3-ply sailmaker's or seine twine or 3-ply linen rug warp

Weft

In this rug, the bulk of the weft is beige cotton muslin, three-quarters of which has been dyed a soft yellow. The inlay blocks are made of corduroy and velvet, some of which were dyed to achieve gradations of color. You can achieve a similar effect by choosing fabrics in like colors.

Take-Up

10 percent in length

Draw-In

8 percent in width

Warping

Wind 220 warp threads in total for a width of 36 inches (91.5 cm) at 6 epi plus two extra threads at each selvage. The rug measures 33 inches (84 cm) wide when off the loom.

Threading & Tie-Up

See the draft. Thread 1–3, 2–3, 1–3, 2–3,... for 16 threads to create the border, then 1–4, 2–4, 1–4, 2–4,... for 12 threads to create the first block, then 1–3, 2–3, 1–3, 2–3,.... for 12 threads to create the second block, then 1–4, 2–4, 1–4, 2–4,... for 12 threads to create the third block, repeat block 1 through block 11 for 15 blocks, ending with 1–3, 2–3, 1–3, 2–3,...for 16 threads to create the other border.

Sleying

6 epi with two extra threads at the selvages

Weft Preparation

Cut or tear fabrics into ⅜-inch (1-cm) strips. If the fabric is very heavy, such as denim, cut narrower strips about ¼ inch (5 mm) wide. If the fabric is very lightweight, such as muslin, cut them a little wider to about ½ inch (1.5 cm).

Weaving

Wind two shuttles for plain weave—one yellow and one beige. Weave a 3-inch (7.5-cm) plain-weave border, treadling 1–2, 3–4, 1–2, 3–4, etc. Weave three rows of yellow and one row of beige to add a bit of richness to the background color. Then lay in the first block using purple rag, treadling **1–3**, 1–2, 3–4, **2–3**, 1–2, 3–4 , etc. The bold type indicates the shed for the pattern weft. Twelve passes of the purple shuttle will complete the purple block. Lay in a little extra plain-weave weft at the edges to compensate for the block inlay. To do so, treadle 1–2, weave to the edge of the block, treadle 3–4, return to the original selvage, treadle 1–2, weave across to the opposite selvage. After the purple block has been completed, go on to a purple and blue mixed weft, treadling **1–4**, 1–2, 3–4, **2–4**, 1–2, 3–4, etc. Continue weaving, following this sequence and changing colors as appropriate to make the blocks. Finish with a 3-inch (7.5-cm) plain-weave border.

Finishing

Make two rows of Damascus edging (see page 80 for details); then darn the warp ends back into the rug.

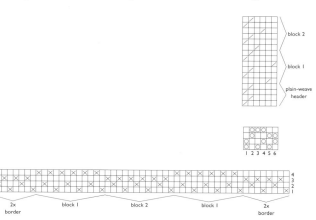

PATCHWORK JEWELS

Design by Jane A. Evans

Rugs like *Patchwork Jewels* look fascinating, are easy to weave, and need only four shafts. Color is their greatest charm. Be wild or restrained; plan carefully or just let it happen. The blocks or patches show as either mostly warp or mostly weft because thick and thin threads alternate in both the warp and the weft. The thin threads hold the thick ones in place, and the thick ones are seen as the colorful patches. The rugs are fully reversible.

The draft has four units, as shown here. Each threading unit holds five threads. The first four threads are all on one shaft and drawn through individual heddles to minimize twisting. These work together as one "thick" end. The fifth or "thin" warp end is on the opposite shaft from that holding the four ends. Shaft 1 is opposite shaft 3, and shaft 2 is opposite shaft 4. Treadling alternates a thick cloth weft with a thin thread weft on opposite treadles. Treadle 1 is opposite treadle 3, and treadle 2 is opposite treadle 4.

A weaver can make endless variations by changing any of these: threading order, or width of the blocks; treadling order, or length of the blocks; weft colors; and frequency of changes. The density of the rug depends on cloth weft size, warp tension, and beat. It is easiest to learn about patchwork rugs by making one; wind a longer warp to weave several variations. The finished size is 29 by 45 inches (73.5 by 114.5 cm).

Equipment & Supplies

Four-shaft four-treadle loom with a weaving width of at least 32 inches (81.5 cm), #12 reed, two stick or ski shuttles (minimum), sewing machine, navy blue cotton sewing thread, liquid fray retardant

Warp

8/4 cotton (1600 yds/lb or 3220 m/kg). You will need 4 ounces (114 g) each of medium blue (MB), red (R), and green (G); 2.2 ounces (62 g) of dark blue (DB); 3.1 ounces (88 g) of lilac (L); and 1.2 ounces (34 g) of purple (P).

Weft

The thin weft is 8/4 cotton (1680 yds/lb or 3380 m/kg), and you will need 2.5 ounces (71 g) of navy. Preshrunk cotton flannel is used for the thick weft, and you will need 30 yards (27.5 m) each of bright blue (BB), dark blue (DB), printed lilac (L), printed red (R), and 20 yd. each of printed green (G), bright green (BG), and purple (P).

Take-up

About 10 percent in length

Draw-in

About 10 percent in width

Warping

Wind a warp of 750 ends, each 7½ feet (2.3 m) long (which allows 30 inches/76 cm of tie-on and loom waste) in color groups as follow: 40 MB, 10 DB, 40 L, 10 R, 40 G, 10 MB, 40 R, 10 DB, 40 DB, 10 G, 40 L, 10 MB, 40 MB, 10 G, 40 P, 10 R, 40 G, 10 R, 40 DB, 10 L, 40 R, 10 G, 40 MB, 10 P, 40 G, 10 R, 40 L, 10 DB, 40 R, and 10 MB. Add two floating selvages of medium blue for neat edges.

Threading & Tie-Up

Beam the warp on one beam to a width of 31¼ inches (79.5 cm). Thread the warp in blocks of 50 threads, each block containing 10 repeats of the units shown in the draft. Start with the 40 MB/10 DB threads and follow this block order: B, C, D, A, D, B, C, D, A, B, C, D, C, A, B. Take four threads from the color group of 40 for the groups of four ends on one shaft; then take one end from the color group of 10 for the single end on one shaft. Repeat

10 times per block. It is all right if the warp ends cross over each other a bit. Tie the treadles as shown in the draft.

Sleying

Sley two ends per dent in a #12 reed for 24 epi.

Weft Preparation

Wash and dry all fabric to preshrink it before cutting it into strips ½ inch (1.5 cm) wide. Wind the fabric strips onto one or more shuttles. Taper and overlap the thick wefts 3 to 4 inches (7.5 to 10 cm) in a shed to make gluing or sewing unnecessary. Wind one shuttle with the 8/4 cotton thread.

Weaving

Using the 8/4 navy cotton weft, weave a hem by alternating treadles 1 and 3, as shown in the draft, for 2½ inches (6.5 cm). Then weave the blocks by alternating a thick cloth weft with an 8/4 weft to total 20 picks per block. Treadle the blocks in the following sequence and color order, referring to the draft as needed: D (L), C (DB), B (R), A (G), D (BB), C (L), A (P), D (BG), C (R), B (DB), A (BB), C (G), B (L), A (R), D (P), C (BG), B (DB), D (BB). Weave the second hem. Advance the warp frequently and avoid extreme tension, which flattens the rug.

Finishing

Apply the fray retardant along the outer ends of both hems before cutting the rug from the loom. Machine-stitch the raw ends well. Turn a ¼-inch (5-mm) hem; then turn the balance of the header in half to abut the thick part of the rug. Machine-stitch the hem near the abutment. Using hot, soapy water, soak the rug in a washing machine, agitate it for one or two minutes, spin, rinse without agitation, and spin again. Lay the rug on a flat surface to dry, blocking it as needed.

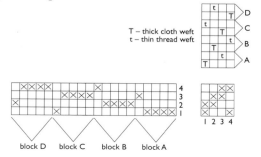

T – thick cloth weft
t – thin thread weft

block D   block C   block B   block A

ICARUS

Design by Sandra von Sneidern

Icarus uses a kilim technique to join a weft-faced plain weave for the background sky and a twill weave for the wing. Weaving this or a similar design is a creative process, where you must find logical methods for dealing with the junctions of the two wefts. On the left side, the twill line is followed; on the right, the line is followed but stepped back two units of twill at regular intervals. It is an exciting process, and sometimes you may not know what to do until you actually do it. That may involve some trial and error at times—this is all part of the creative process. The finished size of the rug is 36 by 44 inches (91.5 by 112 cm).

Equipment

Four-shaft six-treadle loom, #5 reed, several stick shuttles, one optional ski shuttle for the long stretches

Warp

8/3 linen or 12/9 cotton rug warp

Weft

Strips of recycled cotton or polyester fabrics

Take-Up

10 percent in length

Draw-In

10 percent in width

Warping

Wind 224 ends plus 4 selvage ends for a total of 228 ends. Wind the warp two ends at a time, keeping them parallel by placing a finger between the threads. This prevents the threads from twisting around one another and eases the winding on of the warp.

Threading & Tie-Up

See the draft.

Sleying

Sley at 5 epi, one thread per dent, with two ends doubled at each selvage.

Weft Preparation

Collect fabrics in an assortment of darker blues to lighter blues, including some blues that have white spots and some with grey, purple, or brown. For the yellow shades you will need fabrics ranging from light yellow to burnt orange and red-brown. The materials used in *Icarus* included a silk fabric and one with a pink pattern to add a lift of color and a bit of shine. Cut or tear the strips so that when they're tightly twisted, they average the width of a standard pencil. (Adjust the width according to the material used, as described in chapter 4.) When using doubled wefts to allow for color manipulation, the wefts should be half the standard width.

Weaving

Weave a filler, then seven weft shots of a doubled warp yarn in plain weave for the header. Mark the warp with a black waterproof textile marker every 4 inches (10 cm). Using the reed as a guide, mark a light line across the warp. Draw a guide line every 4 inches (10 cm) as far as you can go without advancing the warp. Using another waterproof textile marker in a contrasting color, measure at 2-inch (5-cm) intervals from where the twill line diagonals meet the design center (see figure 1), which is 84 ends from the right selvage. The marks are only a guide. You may find that the angle varies a bit, depending on the width of the strips you use in the twill. Make these guide marks approximately every 8 to 12 inches (20.5 to 30.5 cm) as the warp advances.

The plain-weave border is woven using treadles 1 and 2. The twill area of the wing is woven using treadles 3, 4, 5, and 6. Begin with two sets of doubled wefts, and enter one set from each side. Weave 2 inches (5 cm) of plain weave, varying the colors of one of the wefts in the set to develop various color nuances. Be sure that the weft covers the warp.

After weaving 2 inches of blue plain weave, you are ready to start the twill for the yellow wing area. From this point forward, each area of plain weave is woven separately. On the right, Sandra used two wefts singly, alternating every two plain-weave picks—i.e., filling from the selvage to the twill area and back. One weft is constant, a middle value blue with a touch of brown. The other strip changes from purple to dark blue with white spots and dark grey-blue with a fawn print. On the left side, the border changes from a deep to light blue and eventually becomes the same color as the right side where they blend together again at the top. As you change to a lighter or darker color, you will need to combine two thin wefts of different shades in the same pick, starting both from the outside edge and filling to the twill and back. Always make sure the wefts cover the warp.

In accordance with figure 1, the twill weaving follows the basic twill treadling sequence of 3, 4, 5, 6. Each twill pick is followed by raising the opposite shaft to tuck in the tail of the weft.

Treadle 5 is opposite treadle 3

Treadle 6 is opposite treadle 4

Treadle 3 is opposite treadle 5

Treadle 4 is opposite treadle 6

The twill pick and tuck-in are followed by plain weave, using the meet-and-separate tapestry technique (see page 62) wherever the twill and plain-weave wefts come together. The two wefts pass one another in each shed, which allows for a balanced meeting of the twill and plain weave areas. The diagonal lines of the design prevent the occurrence of the holes that can be problematic with the meet-and-separate technique. Note that each weft starts by passing over the nearest warp end, then crosses over to the other side and ends one warp end past the start of the weft coming from the opposite direction, thus keeping the twill line at an angle. Alternate twill and plain weave so that you have a twill weft at each side of the design and a plain weave weft at each selvage. Using two wefts for the twill allows you to change one at a time for gradual color transitions.

One of the problems you may find is that the build-up becomes uneven between the twill and the plain weave. If this happens, the problem can be adjusted over the next few picks by using a slightly thicker weft or putting in extra wefts. Because the twill wefts are thicker, you can generally weave two plain-weave wefts to one twill, but you must adjust this as the weaving progresses. Keep the plain-weave wefts the same on both sides.

For the jagged edges of the wing, bring the twill weft up seven warp threads inside the opposite twill weft, which will then cross over to the other side in the same shed. Then follow the new twill line, again moving one end out on each pick. This cuts out two twill lines. If you want a deeper cut

for one of your designs, add multiples of four warp threads to the seven above. To cut out only one twill line, as done on the top left side, bring the twill weft up three warp threads inside the opposite twill weft.

When you have woven 27½ inches (70 cm), it is time to start a plain-weave weft at the design center. Treadle 1 and pass one thin weft strip under, over, and under the appropriate warp threads in the middle. Each end can now cross over in the following shed, making two wefts in one pick and leaving a weft end at each side of the twill. Note that the right side follows the twill line, whereas the angle on the left side is much flatter. It may take some ingenuity to work out how to build up the plain weave across the center and to the left. The marks on the warp are only a guide. If necessary, stand up on your loom bench to gain a perspective to see more clearly.

Eventually, as the figure is completed, the plain weave in the center will join that at the sides. Then weave another 2 inches (5 cm) across the top. Finish with a header of doubled warp yarn for seven picks, covering the warp as at the beginning. Insert a few picks of filler to hold the edge in place until you are ready to do the finishing. Cut off the warp about 7 inches (18 cm) from the edge of the piece to provide sufficient length necessary for a woven edge.

Finishing

This rug is completed with finger-woven edges, each ending in a single braid or plait. To keep the edge straight, undo the filler as you weave across the edge. (Refer to chapter 6 for details.)

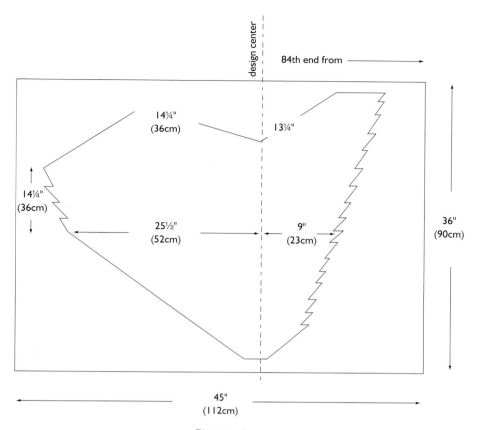

Figure 1

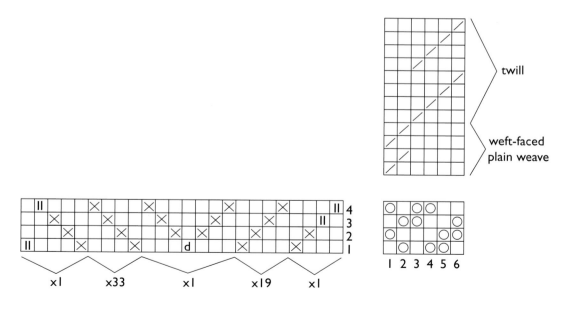

d – design center
ll – doubled ends at selvages

TIDAL CARPET

Design by Missy Stevens

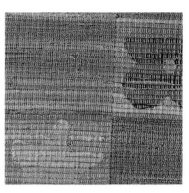

Nongeometric designs are always impressive, and these seaside motifs are especially engaging to anyone who has ever strolled on a beach. Accomplished using the inlay technique, the patterns are simple enough that you needn't be an expert weaver to attempt them. A Shaker-style braided edging completes the rug and neatly frames the design. Its finished size is 32 by 40 inches (81.5 by 101.5 cm).

Equipment & Supplies

Six-shaft four-treadle loom, #18 reed at least 33 inches (84 cm) wide, boat shuttle, four or five paper stencils to use for the inlays, fabric glue

Warp

This rug uses a two-color warp of 5/2 mercerized cotton. The two warp colors should have good value and color contrast, and each color should comprise similar shades—three shades of blue and three shades of soft yellow-gold.

Weft

Strips of clean, recycled corduroy pants in a variety of medium to light blues and soft browns

Take-Up

10 percent in length

Draw-In

Negligible

Warping

Wind a warp of 553 ends, including 42 yellows, 72 blues, 109 yellows and blues, 107 yellows and blues, 109 yellows and blues, 72 blues, and 42 yellows.

Sleying

Sley at one end per dent in a #18 reed for 18 epi; double-sley three dents at each selvage.

Threading & Tie-Up

Thread the 18 epi warp symmetrically in groups: 42 ends of yellow, 72 ends of blue, 109 ends alternating blue and yellow (starting and ending with a yellow end), 107 ends alternating blue and yellow (starting and ending with a yellow end), 109 ends alternating blue and yellow (starting and ending with a yellow end), 72 ends of blue, and 42 ends of yellow. Complete the tie-up as shown in the draft.

Weft Preparation

Cut off the hems from the corduroy pants and rip the fabric from the ankle to the waist, making 1-inch (2.5-cm) strips. Taper both ends of each strip, since the wefts will not be joined but laid in and overlapped. Cut ¼-inch (5-mm) strips in contrasting colors for the inlay patterns. To create the inlay images, use the patterns in figure 1 as a guide to draw and cut paper stencils from graph paper. Use simple shapes that will fit comfortably inside the 6-inch (15-cm) squares of the design. Cut out small triangles in the bottom corners of the pattern squares to act as guides for accurately placing the stencils on the warp while weaving.

Weaving

Weave a 1½-inch (4-cm) plain-weave header in one of the warp colors of 5/2 cotton. Begin weaving, alternately treadling 3 for a shot of rag weft and treadling 4 for a shot of 5/2 mercerized cotton weft. Repeat for seven shots of rag weft or 2 inches (5 cm). Change to a blue block by weaving two consecutive shots of rag weft. Resume alternating the rag weft and 5/2 mercerized cotton. Weave 13 shots of rag weft or 3½ inches (9 cm). Weave one shot of mercerized cotton.

For the inlay design blocks, change to treadle 1 with a shot of rag weft and treadle 2 with a shot of mercerized cotton. This creates two yellow blocks on the sides and one blue block in the center. Lay a stencil on each yellow block to determine where the inlay designs should begin. Weave until you reach the shot where the inlay begins; then put in your weft rag shot as usual and beat, but don't change the shed. Lay the stencil on top of the warp and cut narrow inlay strips to fit, taking care not to cut any warp threads! Leave the strips in place and remove the stencil. Open the shed and position the first strip on top of the rag weft shot and under the warp. Continue this procedure until the first row of blocks is complete—about 20 shots of rag weft or 6 inches (15 cm).

Change rows (blocks) by weaving two consecutive rag shots, shifting to a pattern of one yellow block in the center with one blue block on each side. Proceed as before with the stencil and inlay design in the center yellow block.

Repeat this procedure for a total of five rows of blocks, creating eight inlay images.

Weave a shot of mercerized cotton. Repeat the beginning border: sing treadle 4, weave with a shot of rag weft; then treadle 3 with the mercerized cotton for a total of 13 rag weft shots or 3½ inches (9 cm). Change colors by weaving two consecutive rag weft shots. Treadle 3 with one shot of rag weft and treadle 4 with a shot of mercerized cotton for a total of seven rag weft shots or 2 inches (5 cm). Weave a 1½-inch (4-cm) plain-weave header of mercerized cotton.

Before removing the rug from the loom, run a bead of fabric glue along the edges of the header, placing the glue slightly away from the body of the rug. After the glue has dried, cut off the rug.

Finishing

Finish the rug by weaving a four-strand braid of corduroy strips. (Refer to chapter 6 for details on making a four-strand braid.) Experiment with color combinations until you find a balance that complements the rug. Fold the header back and stitch it down on the reverse side of the rug; then hand-stitch the braid to the edge of the rug, overlapping the ends.

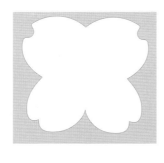

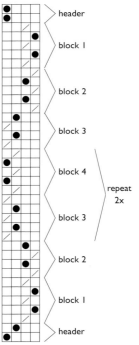

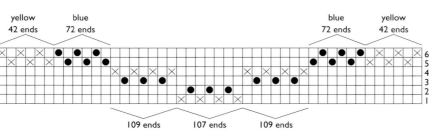

● – blue
✕ – yellow

Seamist II

Design by Jutta Graf

This rug is woven in a six-block weave. Jutta custom-dyes all of her materials used in the warp and weft, however commercial fabric can be substituted in similar shades or entirely different color combinations. It may be fun to try different fabrics, such as prints. *Seamist* is reversible with a subtly shaded random-weave effect on the "wrong" side. Since there are four to five wefts in each pick, the rug is very thick and sturdy. The finished size is 32 by 51 inches (81.5 by 129.5 cm).

Equipment

Eight-shaft eight-treadle loom, #8 reed at least 36 inches (91.5 cm) wide, nine 25-inch (63.5-cm) ski shuttles, one 13-inch (33-cm) boat shuttle

Warp

12/9 cotton in white, black, aqua, and yellow

Weft

100 percent cotton in light gray, true red, fuchsia, green, orange, purple, pale yellow, moss green and hot pink. Gray chenille and scrap cotton yarn in a single color are used for the headers.

Take-Up

20 percent in length

Draw-In

10 percent in width

Warping

Wind 268 ends, each 3 yards (2.7 m) long; this includes take-up and 27 inches (68.5 cm) loom waste. Jutta used different colors for each block, alternating white for the pattern thread and a color for the tie-down thread. To create a slightly different effect, try using only one color instead.

Threading & Tie-Up

See the draft.

Sleying

One end per dent except at both selvages, where the first four dents are double sleyed.

Weft Preparation

Jutta hand-dyes cotton sheets to obtain a wide range of colors before cutting them into 1-inch (2.5-cm) strips.

Weaving

Thread a floating selvage with linen. Weave 3 to 4 inches (7.5 to 10 cm) of filler; then weave a ½-inch (1.5-cm) header, using the scrap cotton yarn. Following the treadling instructions in the draft, begin weaving with light gray and true red cotton strips, taking care to start the shuttles from the opposite sides of the web. Beat firmly after each pick. After completing the first four picks, continue the plain weave with chenille. Follow the treadling instructions to complete the rug. Weave a ½-inch (1.5-cm) header in plain weave, using the cotton yarn. Allow 8 inches (20.5 cm) of warp at each end for the fringe.

Finishing

Remove the scrap filler strips at the beginning of the rug and make a braided fringe at both ends. Wash the rug in the washing machine, set on a gentle cycle with warm water; then block the damp rug and allow it to air dry.

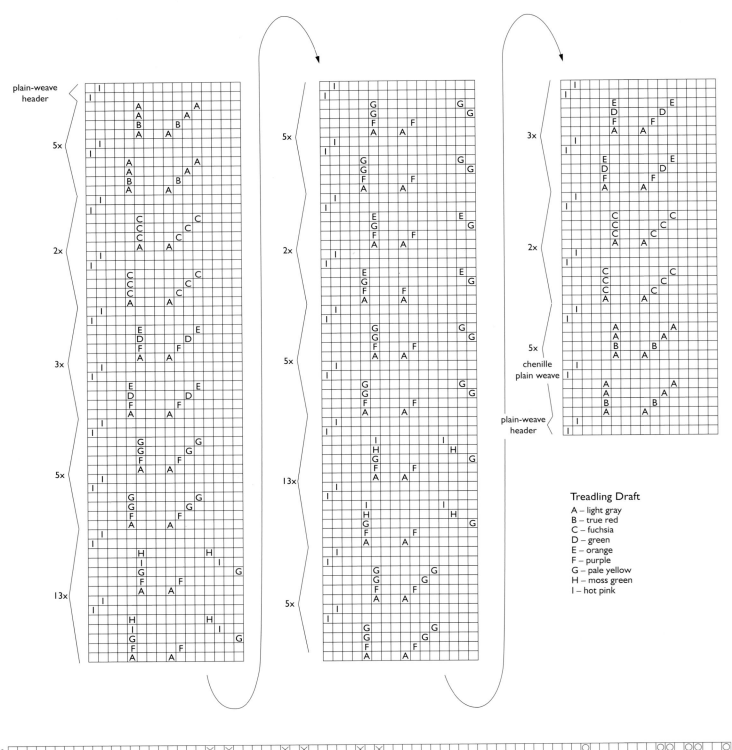

Treadling Draft

A – light gray
B – true red
C – fuchsia
D – green
E – orange
F – purple
G – pale yellow
H – moss green
I – hot pink

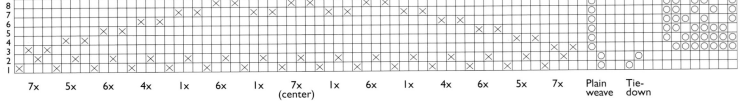

RUG NUMBER 35A

Design by Jane Doyle

In this rug, woven in Summer and Winter, the large basket-weave pattern appears in opposite colors on each side. Its limited palette provides an excellent opportunity to experiment with color combinations that produce a variety of effects. You can create a rug where the stripes appear to vibrate, where one color dominates the other, or where the stripes are hardly visible. Although it looks complicated in appearance, this rug weaves up very nicely. The finished size is 38 by 69 inches (96.5 by 175 cm).

Equipment

Eight-shaft 12-treadle loom with a weaving width of at least 48 inches (122 cm), #8 reed 48 inches (122 cm) long, one boat shuttle, eight rag shuttles, sewing machine

Warp

8/4 cotton carpet warp, 1200 yards (1097 m) each of dark brown and light teal green

Weft

300 yards (274 m) each of purple and chocolate brown fabric that is cut on the bias into strips 1½ inch (4 cm) wide, brown or purple thread

Take-Up

About 5.5 percent in length

Draw-In

12 percent in width

Warping

Warp at 16 epi. Eight working ends are doubled sleyed. Warp calculation is: 16 ends × 43 inches wide + 4 (floating selvages) = 692 ends × 3 yards length = 2076 yards + 100 yards for weaving the header = 2176 yards (1990 m) total warp. Double warp the 16 epi to make 8 working ends per inch. Wind on the two warp colors together when warping.

Sleying

Double-sley the two warp colors together through each dent and heddle. Leave the first two and the last two ends as floating selvages, threading them through the reed but not through the heddles.

Threading & Tie-Up

See the draft.

Weft Preparation

If possible, cut the 1½-inch (4-cm) weft strips on the bias, as they pack better. Straight-cut rags may be used instead, but they will produce a different effect.

Weaving

This weave structure produces two layers. Because shafts 1 and 2 are tie-downs, they lie between the two layers and do not show. The remaining shafts are pattern shafts. Therefore, although shafts 1 and 2 are shown in the draft, the true pattern will look different because the warp from those two shafts will be hidden in the rug. Similarly, when treadling this weave, you need four tie-ups for each block, and each lift must be combined with shaft 1 or 2. In addition, the two shafts are treadled on opposites. For example, a block would be thus:

Treadles 1 and 7 will raise shafts 1 and 3–4–5 purple

Treadles 1 and 8 will raise shafts 1 and 6–7–8 brown

Treadles 2 and 7 will raise shafts 2 and 3–4–5 purple

Treadles 2 and 8 will raise shafts 2 and 6–7–8 brown

To simplify the tie-up and use fewer treadles (this rug would require 20 treadles otherwise), Jane ties shafts 1 and 2 separately, then ties the pattern shafts in the combinations shown in the draft.

To begin weaving, wind two warp colors together on a bobbin. Using a boat shuttle, weave a 2-inch (5-cm) header. Since there is no true plain weave in this pattern, use shafts 1 and 7 together against shafts 2 and 8 (raising shafts 1–3–4–5 and 2–6–7–8)

For the body of the rug, treadle 1 together with treadle 3 (shafts 3–4–5–6–7–8) and throw the purple shuttle from the right, being sure to go under the floating selvage. Then treadle 1 and treadle 4 (no shaft) and throw a brown shuttle from the left, going under the floating selvage when entering the shed and going over the floating selvage on the way out. A little reminder note or diagram tacked to the loom castle can help. Next, treadle 2 and 3 and throw the purple shuttle; then treadle 2 and 4 and throw the brown shuttle. This completes one block, which in this case is all purple on the top and all brown on the underside. Continue throwing the shuttles in this sequence for the entire rug, finishing with 2 inches (5 cm) of plain-weave header. In the draft, each square equals 1 inch (2.5 cm).

Finishing

Carefully cut the finished rug from the loom. Using the sewing machine, stay-stitch the raw ends of the header so that they won't unravel. Fold one-third of the header toward the body of the rug and sew twice. Fold it over again, aligning the edge of the hem with the edge of the body of the rug; then sew twice, making sure to backstitch and reinforce the ends. Trim any stray weft tails protruding from the body of the rug.

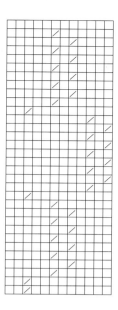

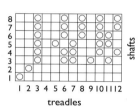

treadles

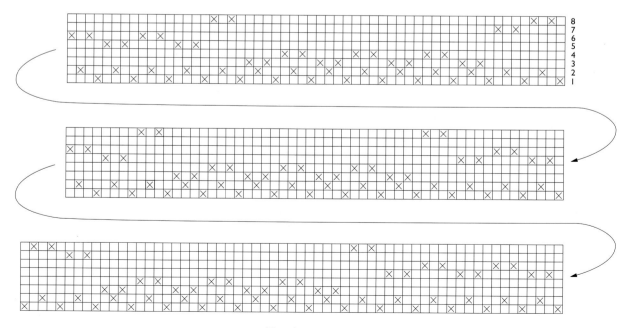

Threading

119

VIII
CARE OF RAG RUGS

Depending on where a rag rug is located in the home—on the floor, on the wall, in a secluded area, or in a major hallway—it should be thoroughly cleaned and aired at least once a year. During the interim, vacuuming or sweeping is an effective way to remove surface dirt. Vacuum or sweep both the right and wrong sides.

▼

Rag rugs should not be shaken, as this puts a considerable amount of stress on the warp. When holding or hanging a rug, make sure to grasp the selvages rather than the ends. In this position, the strong weft fabric—not the weaker warp thread—is the support.

There is one very effective, old-fashioned way to get rid of the dust and dirt that settles into a rag rug over time. Lay the rug over a railing with the selvages lying parallel to the ground. Using a carpet beater, gently beat out the dust and dirt. Let the dust settle; then flip the rug and repeat. This should be done on a porch or exterior railing, as it can produce a lot of dust.

Washing

Before washing your rug, make sure all the fabrics in the rug are color fast. If you are uncertain, stick to vacuuming or a cold water wash. Also check the rug for wear or damage; if you find any weak areas or broken warp threads, darn or mend them.

Small rugs may be washed in a washing machine on a gentle cycle with warm water, then blocked and air dried. Large rugs and those that you don't want to put through the rigors of the washing machine can be laundered in a bathtub with warm, soapy water. Large rugs may be folded to lie flat in the tub, but make sure to rearrange and agitate them often. Change the water during the washing process, if necessary. Rag rugs can become very heavy when they're wet; to handle them, roll or loosely fold the rug in the same fashion as it was rolled on the loom. Once you have finished laundering it, lay the rug over a bucket or two and allow the excess water to drain off. This facilitates either blocking or air drying.

If you live in a colder area, you can follow in the Scandinavian tradition of laying your rug out on fresh, clean snow. Cover the rug with additional clean snow. When you sweep off the snow, it will take the dust and dirt along with it. Using this method, a rug can be cleaned and aired simultaneously.

There is a still a strong outdoor laundering tradition in the Scandinavian countries, especially during the spring and fall, directly after and before the long winter. Rag rugs are washed in the lakes and rivers with good, strong soap and scrubbed with sturdy brushes. In Sweden there are special washing houses, and Finland has special docks and racks for washing and drying rag rugs along its many lake shores.

For those of us who don't have lake-front property or beautiful clean snow, a flat driveway will work fine. Larger rugs can be laid on the driveway and soaked with a garden hose. Using good soap and a

brush, scrub the rug thoroughly on both sides. Rinse well with the hose and spread the rug flat or hang it by the selvages to air dry. While it is still slightly damp, the rug can be blocked if necessary. (Refer to chapter 6.)

Rag rugs become softer and more worn over time. On many rag rugs, the warp wears out, but the rags are as good as they were the day they were originally woven. Historically rag rugs were often disassembled and the rags rewoven on a fresh warp to make a revitalized rug. This practice is still in use today.

Analogous colors: Colors that are closely related to each other and generally lie next to each other on the color wheel. Often used in groups of three or four, they are low in contrast and therefore blend well.

Apron: A canvas fabric that connects the tie-on bar to the cloth beam of the loom. There may also be an apron on the warp beam.

Back beam: A rigid beam at the back of the loom that supports the warp and maintains its horizontal position

Balanced weave: A weave in which the number of warp threads per inch is equal to the number of weft threads per inch

Beaming: The process of winding the warp threads onto the warp beam of the loom

Beater: The framework that supports the reed on a loom. It swings freely to pack the weft into position.

Blocking: The process of moistening and shaping handwoven textiles so that they conform to the desired shape

Block weave: Any of several weave structures that produce patterns based on squares or rectangles

Bobbin: A spool or quill around which warp thread is wound for weaving. Often the bobbin fits into a shuttle.

Bobbin winder: A simple hand-cranked or electric tool for winding thread or yarn onto a bobbin, spool, or quill

Bound weave: A weft-faced twill using multiple colors of weft. On the reverse side, the pattern and colors are the opposite of those on the face.

Brake: A mechanism on the warp beam and the cloth beam that prevents them from turning. When engaged, the brake holds the warp under tension; it is released to advance the warp.

Castle: The upright framework that supports the shafts

Catalogne: Canadian term for bed coverings that are woven using weft made of strips of wool or cotton cloth

Chaining: The process of looping the warp upon itself to prevent it from tangling during its transfer from the warping frame to the loom

Choke ties: Lengths of cord wrapped tightly around the warp threads immediately after warping to maintain the order of the warp during its transfer to the loom

Cloth beam: A beam at the front of the loom onto which the finished cloth is wound as it is woven

Cloutie: Scottish term for rag-woven coverlets

Contrast: A dissimilarity between two or more colors. Value contrast is based on the relative lightness or darkness of the colors being compared; color contrast is based on their relative positions on the color wheel.

Complementary colors: Colors that are opposite each other on the color wheel, such as red and green or purple and yellow. Complementary colors create the strongest possible color contrast, and when placed in close proximity, each intensifies the appearance of the other.

Counterbalanced loom: A floor loom in which the shafts operate in tandem—as one shaft is raised, the connecting one is lowered. It is also called a sinking-shed loom. This type of loom cannot weave twills and other more complex designs.

Countermarche loom: A floor loom in which the shafts can be pulled up or down independently

Couvertures de marriage: Bridal coverlets that were an integral part of dowries in Acadian areas, notably in eastern Canada and Louisiana

Crackle weave: A four-shaft block weave similar to Summer and Winter

Cross: The point at which the warp threads meet each other coming and going around the pegs on the warping frame. The cross maintains the correct sequence of the threads.

Cross ties: These preliminary ties, which are applied to the warp when it is on the warping frame, maintain the cross until the lease sticks are inserted.

Dent: Each slot in the reed. The dents are used for spacing the warp.

Double binding: A very sturdy Swedish rug-weaving pattern that is reversible and generally woven in a block or plaid design. It is a type of double-faced weave.

Double-faced weave: A single warp that is woven with two sets of wefts that appear on the opposite sides of the rug.

Double sleying: The process of placing two warp threads through each dent in the reed

Draft: A graphic representation, usually done on graph paper or a computer screen, of the mechanics of a particular weave, including the threading, treadling, and tie-up

Draw device: A supplemental warp-lifting mechanism that allows the weaver to lift certain threads in addition to the threaded and treadled design; a standardized way to create a pick-up design on a floor loom

Draw-in: The amount of shrinkage across the width of the rug. It is caused by the weft tension created during the weaving process.

Dressing: Preparation of the loom for weaving, including beaming, threading the heddles, sleying the reed, and tying on to the front apron

Drugget: A rug generally stripped with a cotton warp and a wool weft

Ear: A short end of the weft that protrudes from the surface of a woven rug

End: Individual warp thread

Fell line: The front or forward edge of your weaving; the edge made by the most recent weft shot

Filler: Rows of heavy waste yarn or rags that are used at the beginning of a new warp to spread it evenly. It is also used between rugs to reserve a length of warp for making fringe.

Filling: See weft.

Float: The portion of a warp or weft that extends without intersection across two or more threads

Floating selvage: One or more warp threads at the selvage that are not threaded through the heddles. These help the rug lie flat.

Frame loom: A simple square or rectangular loom, usually lacking shafts and a beater

Grist: The size or thickness of a thread

Guide string: A preliminary measuring cord used to establish the correct warp length and pattern of winding on the warping frame

Hand: The touch or feel of a fabric

Harness: A set of shafts that performs a given function on a loom

Heddle: A wire or string cord with an eye in the center. One or more warp yarns are threaded through each heddle to control the systematic separation of the warp and create a shed.

Heddle hook: A tool for threading warp threads through the heddles prior to weaving

Hit and Miss: The woven pattern resulting from randomly sewing strips together; also called Hit or Miss

Hue: The pure state of any color

Inlay: A finger-manipulated weave in which short weft strips in contrasting colors are laid in the shed on top of the ground weave to create decorative patterns

Intensity: The relatively purity or grayness of a color

Interlocking weft: A tapestry technique in which the two wefts wrap around each other (as opposed to the kilim or meet-and-separate technique)

Jack loom: A floor loom in which each shaft operates independently. The shafts rise when the treadles are depressed, and it is also called a rising-shed loom.

Kilim: A tapestry technique in which areas of color are created by individual wefts. It is also referred to as slit tapestry, since the wefts never interlock, and vertical slits are created in some designs.

Kotatsugake: A Japanese rag-woven or quilted cloth that is placed over a kotatsu, a low table that contains a heating element.

Laid-in weave: See inlay.

Lamm: A bar that connects the individual shafts to the appropriate treadles. The connections can be changed according to the weave pattern desired.

Lease sticks: A pair of smooth wooden slats that are used to maintain the cross in the warp yarns during the beaming on and threading process

List: A narrow strip of material or fabric selvage. Colonial rag rugs were often referred to as list carpets.

Loom: Any device used for weaving that can hold the warp threads under tension and in their proper positions

Loom-controlled weave: Any weave that is created solely through the interaction of the heddles and the shafts on a loom

Loom waste: The unweavable portion of the warp threads required for tying on to the loom and cut off at the end of the weaving process; also called thrums

Over dyeing: The process of dyeing a second color over a previous one

Pawl: A catch lever of a ratchet that prevents backward motion

Pick: See shot.

Pick count: The number of weft shots per inch in a woven fabric; also called picks per inch

Plain weave: A basic weave of one up and one down in both the warp and weft; also called tabby

Plying: The process of twisting two or more strands of yarn or strips of cloth together

Popanna: A Finnish style of cutting rag weft on the bias to allow for greater drape in blankets or clothing

Primary color: A color that cannot be mixed from any other color. The three primary colors are red, yellow, and blue.

Quill: A bobbin used to hold weft thread. The quill fits inside a larger shuttle. Originally the spine of a feather was used for this purpose, but today a quill often consists of a tube of heavy paper.

Raddle: A narrow, flat board with nails or pegs protruding at regular 1- or 2-inch (2.5- or 5-cm) intervals. It is used to distribute the warp evenly across the loom while the warp is being wound.

Ratchet: See brake.

Reed: A metal device, similar to a large comb, that is set into the beater on a loom. The reed helps to space and maintain the horizontal position of the warp threads and to beat each new weft shot into position. It is numbered according to how many dents per inch it contains and is available in numerous sizes and lengths.

Reed hook: A short S-shaped hook used in sleying or drawing the warp through the reed prior to weaving; also called a sley hook

Rep weave: A warp-faced weave

Resist: Any material that is applied to a surface before dyeing or printing to prevent absorption of the dye into the covered or resisted area

Ripsmatta: A warp-faced plain weave, Scandinavian in origin, that uses thick and thin wefts to produce a rib effect

Rolakan: A Scandinavian term for tapestry

Saki-ori: A cloth made with a rag weft, also known by a number of other names in various areas of Japan

Scouring: A thorough cleaning that removes dirt and oils from fabrics. Fabrics are always scoured before dyeing.

Secondary color: The product of mixing two primary colors; i.e., green, orange, and purple

Sectional beam: A back beam or warp beam with pegs set at 1- or 2-inch (2.5- or 5-cm) intervals to allow for sectional warping

Sectional warping: A warping method in which warp threads are wound directly from spools onto one section at a time of the sectional beam of a loom

Selvage: The lengthwise or warpwise edge of woven fabric; the point at which the weft binds the warp to form a finished edge

Sett: The number of warp thread or ends per inch in the reed, which determines the density of the warp of a fabric

Shaft: The internationally used term for the frame that supports a group of heddles on the loom (also called a harness in the United States). A group of shafts working together is referred to as a harness.

Shed: The space between raised or lowered warp yarns through which a loaded shuttle is passed. A shed is created by raising or lowering one or more shafts.

Shot: One pass or row of weft through a shed; also called a pick

Shuttle: A tool on which the weft is wrapped so that it can be passed through a shed in the warp

Silkscreen printing: A form of stencil printing in which dye or textile ink is squeezed through a stretched mesh of silk that has a stencil or resist applied to create a design

Single sley: One warp threaded through each dent in the reed

Sley hook: See reed hook.

Sleying: The process of drawing the warp yarns through the reed on a loom

Slip knot: A temporary knot made to be unfastened easily; also called a noose knot

Stretcher: See temple.

String heddle: A heddle made of sturdy string, having an eye in the center. A string heddle can be added to hold a warp threaded that was inadvertently missed during threading.

Summer and Winter: A double-sided block weave with interior plain-weave tie-down warp threads. It is generally used to create geometric block-based designs.

Tabby: See plain weave.

Tails: See ears.

Take-up: The amount of extra warp needed to accommodate the over-and-under curvature caused by the rag weft

Tapestry: A weave in which sections of weft are often discontinuous. It is used to create decorative or expressive designs.

Taqueté: A Scandinavian form of pick-up or hand-manipulated Summer-and-Winter weave

Tatter weave: Continuous inlay of a supplemental weft

Temple: An adjustable tool with prongs or nails on each end. It is used for maintaining a consistent width of fabric while weaving

Tension: The tautness of warp yarns. The amount of tension on the loom should equal that created during the measuring process.

Tension box: A device for maintaining the warp tension during sectional warping

Tertiary color: A color produced by combining two secondary colors or one secondary and one primary color. These are generally browns or earth tones.

Threading hook: See heddle hook.

Thrums: Any short length of yarn, including loom waste

Tie-on bar: A metal rod to which the warp is tied. Both the front and back of the loom may have a tie-on bar.

Tie-up: The connections between the shafts and the lamms and between the lamms and the treadles on a floor loom. Tie-up is also the process of making the connections for a particular weave structure.

Treadles: Foot pedals or levers that raise or lower the shafts on a floor loom

Twill: A basic weave characterized by a diagonal effect. Reverse twills can form herringbone and diamond effects.

Value: The lightness or darkness of a color

Warp: A set of threads that are parallel to each other and to the selvage; the lengthwise element in a woven construction:

Warp-faced weave: A fabric or rug in which the warp predominates, completely covering the weft

Warping: The process of preparing the warp for beaming on the loom, including measuring, establishing the cross, and chaining

Warping frame: A simple wooden frame used for measuring the warp before it is beamed on to the loom. Pegs are attached at appropriate locations to facilitate winding, set the length of the warp, and establish the cross.

Warping mill: A device for measuring warps. In contrast to a warping frame, a mill rotates, thus saving your arm the back-and-forth motion required with a frame. A warping mill is faster and more efficient for measuring out long warps.

Warping pegs: Individual pegs that are clamped to stationary surfaces to hold the warp. The pegs are positioned the desired distance apart to obtain the required warp length.

Warping reel: See warping mill.

Weave: The particular pattern in which the warp and the weft come together

Weaving: The process by which a warp and a weft are interlaced at right angles to form a continuous fabric

Web: The fabric created by interlacing warp and weft; the product of the loom

Weft: The set of strips of cloth or yarns perpendicular to the selvage; the horizontal or crosswise elements of a woven construction; also called filling, picks, and woof

Weft-faced weave: A fabric or rug in which the weft dominates and completely covers the warp

CONTRIBUTING ARTISTS

Wendy Bateman
Box 269 Haliburton
Ontario, KOMA1SO Canada

Lis Bech
Højbovænge 12
DK 3500 Værløse Denmark

Liv Bugge
Årvollveien 7
N-0590 Oslo Norway

Kveta Cholvadová
Liptovska Kokava, Slovakia

Johanna Erickson
48 Chester Street
Watertown, Massachusetts 02172
USA

Jane A. Evans
Box 129
Grandora, SK SOK 1V0 Canada

Jutta Graf
RR 1 Box 517
Deer Isle, Maine 04627 USA

Carmen Grier
Penland School
Penland, North Carolina 28765
USA

Suzanne Grinnan
287 Conway Road
South Deerfield, Massachusetts
01373 USA

Judi Gunter
RR 2
Belwood, Ontario
NOB 1J0 Canada

Chad Alice Hagen
Asheville, North Carolina USA

Beth Hatton
171 Trafalgar Street
Annandale, NSW 2038 Australia

Gullvi Heed
Glafsereds Gård
516 95 Målsryd, Sweden

Claudia Olson Hicks
19516 5th Avenue South
Des Moines, Washington 98148
USA

Helga Höhne
Kopenhagener Str. 43
104 37 Berlin, Germany

Sara Hotchkiss
24 Hanson Street
Portland, Maine 04103 USA

Karen Olesen Jakse
8820 Hidden Oaks Drive
Eden Prairie, Minnesota 55344 USA

Susan Johnson
Route 3, Box 171
Viroqua, Wisconsin 54665 USA

Catherine K
78 Ebden Street
Ainslie ACT 2602 Australia

Hanna Korvela
Minna Canthin Katu 20-22
70100 Kuopio, Finland

Chiyoko Kumon
2-44 Fiukatanicho
Nishinomiya, Hyogo
7662 Japan

Lorraine Lamothe
Australian Capital Territory,
Australia

Sara Ann Lindsay
31 Mary Street
North Hobart Tasmania
7000 Australia

Jackie Mackay
RR5
Berwick, Nova Scotia
Canada BOP IEO

Wynne Mattila
3509 East 26th Street
Minneapolis, Minnesota 55406 USA

Claudia Mills
5 Brewer Street
Jamaica Plain, Massachusetts 02130
USA

Alison Milne
9 Wood Bay Road
Titirangi Auckland 7 New Zealand

Alison Morton
Eagles Yard
Machynlleth
Powys SY20 8AG England

Ingela Norén
83 Ridge Road
Westtown, New York 10998 USA

Viveka Nygren
Älgkärr
71995 Vintrosa Sweden

Eva Nyhus
Veveriet RuterDame AS
Hasdalgata 20
4950 Risør Norway

Antónia Raposová
Hubová, Slovakia

Wendy Regier
RR 1 Box 10
Proctorsville, Vermont 05153 USA

Raili Ruppa
Haapatie 5A2
FI-40800 Vaajakoski Finland

Nadine Sanders
P.O. Box 268
Chehalis, Washington 98532 USA

Debra Sharpee
W5472 Wangsness Road
DeForest, Wisconsin 53532 USA

Margaret Shaw
12846 Pleasant Lake Road
Manchester, Michigan 48158 USA

Valeska Siddall
3 Tytherleigh Street
Wanniassa ACT 2903 Australia

Sheree White Sorrells
84 North Main Street
Waynesville, North Carolina 28786
USA

Missy Stevens
Washington, Connecticut USA

Shirley Tommos
Eketorpsvägen 21
S-18261 Djursholm Sweden

Sandra von Sneidern
P.O. Box 93
Braidwood
NSW 2622 Australia

Gisela von Weisz
Stallbacken 5
S-18161 Lidingö Sweden

Mary Anne Wise
N 301 250th Street
Stockholm, Wisconsin 54769 USA

ADDITIONAL RESOURCES

Most larger towns and cities have shops that sell a variety of weaving materials and equipment. Consult your local telephone directory for stores near you. In addition, the periodicals listed below are valuable sources of information on looms, warp, weft, and other supplies. Your local library can also recommend other sources.

CraftNews
Ontario Crafts Council
35 McCaul St.
Toronto, Ontario M5T 1V7
Canada
(416) 977-3551

Crafts
Crafts Council
44A Pentonville Road
London N1 9BY England
(0171) 278 7700

Fiberarts
Altamont Press
50 College Street
Asheville, North Carolina 28801
(704) 253-0467

Form Function Finland
Finnish Society of Crafts and Design/Design Forum Finland
Fabianinkatu 10
FIN-00130 Helsinki
Finland
358-0-6220 8114

Handwoven
Interweave Press
201 East Fourth Street
Loveland, Colorado 80537
(970) 669-7672

International Textilkunst
M. & H. Schaper GmbH & Co.
Postfach 1642
31061 Alfeld
Germany
(0 51 81) 81 09-0

Shuttle Spindle & Dyepot
The Handweavers Guild of America, Inc.
2402 University Avenue, Suite 702
St. Paul, Minnesota 55114-1701
(612) 646-0802

Surface Design Journal
Surface Design Association
P.O. Box 20799
Oakland, CA 94620-0799
(707) 829-3110

Textile Fibre Forum
The Australian Forum for Textile Arts (TAFTA)
P.O. Box 38
The Gap
Q4061 Australia
07-3300-6491

VÄV Magasinet
Svarspost
Kundnummer 290021800
S - 280 64 Glimakra
Sweden
044-427 30

The Weaver's Friend
A Publication for Rag Rug Weavers
5672 North Shore Drive
Duluth, Minnesota 55804
(218) 525-5778

Weaver's
P.O. Box 1525
Sioux Falls, South Dakota 57101-1525
1(800) 232-5648

BIBLIOGRAPHY

Arrow, Jan. *By Southern Hands: a Celebration of Craft Traditions in the South.* Birmingham, Alabama: Roundtable Press, 1987.

Atwater, Mary M. *Hand Woven Rugs.* Santa Ana, CA: HTH Publishers, 1948.

Bayles, David and Ted Orland. *Art & Fear.* Santa Barbara, California: Capra Press, 1993

Brill, Maria L. "Rag Rugs." *Cairo Today* (November 1983): 66–68.

Burnham, Harold B. and Dorothy K. Burnham. *Keep Me Warm One Night: Early Handweaving in Eastern Canada.* Toronto: University of Toronto Press, 1972.

Collingwood, Peter. *Techniques of Rug Weaving.* New York: Watson-Guptill, 1968.

Collingwood, Peter. *Rug Weaving Techniques: Beyond the Basics.* Loveland, Colorado: Interweave Press, 1990.

Fredlund, Jane and Brigit Wiberg. *Rag Rug Weaves: Patterns from Sweden.* Stockholm: LTS Forlag, 1986.

Glasgow, Vaughn L. "Textiles of the Louisiana Acadians," *The Magazine Antiques,* vol. CXX, no. 2 (August 1981): 338–348.

Gordon, Beverly. *Shaker Textile Arts.* Hanover, New Hampshire: University Press of New England, 1980.

Harvey, Anne-Charlotte Hanes. *Swedish Handcraft.* New York: Van Nostrand Reinhold, 1977.

Hauge, Victor and Takako. *Folk Traditions in Japanese Art.* New York: Van Nostrand Reinhold, 1977.

Herald, Jacqueline. *World Crafts: A Celebration of Designs and Skills.* Asheville, North Carolina: Lark Books, 1993.

Hinchcliffe, John and Angela Jeffs. *Rugs from Rags.* Chatsworth, California: Brooke House Publishers, 1977.

Itten, Johannes. *The Elements of Color.* New York: Van Nostrand Reinhold, 1970.

Jackson, Carole. *Color Me Beautiful.* New York: Ballantine Books, 1980.

Johnson, Geraldine Niva. *Weaving Rag Rugs; A Women's Craft in Western Maryland.* Knoxville, Tennessee: University of Knoxville Press, 1985.

Katoh, Amy Sylvester. *Japan Country Living: Spirit, Tradition, Style.* Rutland, VT: Charles E. Tuttle, 1993.

Krook, Inga. "From Rags to Riches." *Handwoven,* vol. IV, no. 3 (Summer 1983): 32–38.

Lewes, Klares, and Helen Hutton. *Rug Weaving.* Newton Center, MA: Charles T. Branford, 1962.

Landreau, Anthony N. *America Underfoot: A History of Floor Coverings from Colonial Times to the Present.* Washington, D.C.: Smithsonian Institution Press, 1976.

Ligon, Linda C., ed. *A Rug Weaver's Sourcebook.* Loveland, Colorado: Interweave Press, 1984.

Little, Nina Fletcher. *Floor Coverings in New England Before 1850.* Sturbridge, MA: Old Sturbridge Village, 1967.

Meany, Janet and Paula Pfaff. *Rag Rug Handbook.* Saint Paul: Dos Tejedoras Fiber Arts Publications, 1988.

Renken, Arlene Helen. *Symbolic Ethnicity in the Rag Rug Weaving Craft of Finnish Americans.* Ph.D. dissertation, University of Wisconsin-Madison, 1986.

Rossetter, Tabitha Wilson. "The Acadian Textile Heritage," *Fiberarts,* vol. 8 no. 3 (May/June 1981): 29–32.

Roth, Rodris. *Floor Coverings in 18th-Century America.* Washington, D.C.: Smithsonian Institution Press, 1967.

Spring, Christopher and Julie Hudson. *North African Textiles.* Washington, D.C.: Smithsonian Institution Press, 1995.

Sutton, Ann and Diane Sheehan. *Ideas in Weaving.* Loveland, CO: Interweave Press, 1989.

Tod, Osma Gallinger and Josephine Couch Del Deo. *Designing and Making Handwoven Rugs.* New York: Dover Publications, 1976.

United States Tariff Commission. *Rag Rugs: Report of the United States Tariff Comission to the President of the United States.* Washington, DC: U.S. Government Printing Office, 1928.

Johansson, Lillemor and Pia Wedderien and Marie Rolander, eds. *Swedish Rag Rugs: 35 New Designs.* Glimakra, Sweden: Forlags AB Vavhasten, 1995.

Von Rosensteil, Helene. *American Rugs and Carpets.* New York: William Morrow, 1978.

Walter, Judy Anne. *Creating Color: A Dyer's Handbook.* Evanston, IL: Cooler by the Lake Publications, 1989

Weinblatt, Victor. "The American Rag Carpet: A Rags-to-Riches Story." *Country Living* (November, 1985): 138–139, 156–158.

Weltge, Sigrid Wortmann. *Women's Work: Textile Art from the Bauhaus.* San Francisco: Chronicle Books, 1993.

Wilson, Kax. *A History of Textiles.* Boulder, Colorado: Westview Press, 1979.

Yoshida, Shin-Ichiro and Dai Williams. *Riches from Rags: Saki-Ori & Other Recycling Traditions in Japanese Rural Clothing.* Tokyo: Audrey Design, 1994.

SUBJECT INDEX

PROJECTS

ACKNOWLEDGMENTS

I wish to thank the wonderful weavers, many included in this book, all of whom responded enthusiastically to my inquires on rag rug weaving. Without their energy, this book could not have been written. A book cannot be written without a strong support group, and gratitude is expressed to Faye and Winslow Eaves, Jane and Paul Anderson, Ute Bargmann, Dai Williams, Claudia Mills, Ruth Gaynes, Catherine Muerdter, Gregg Johnson, Susan Leveille, and many others. I would also like to thank Michael Rouse and Suzanne Grinnan, who were invaluable for emotional support and editing, and my wonderful family especially my mom, Marion Allen, who has always supported me in my endeavors. For their assistance with location photography, thanks go to Patti Hill, Mona Reed, and Thais Wiener. Thanks also to Rob Pulleyn, Leslie Dierks, Dana Irwin, and the staff at Lark Books.